→INTRODUCING

EVOLUTIONARY PSYCHOLOGY

DYLAN EVANS & OSCAR ZARATE

This edition published in
the UK and the USA
in 2010 by Icon Books Ltd,
Omnibus Business Centre,
39–41 North Road, London N7 9DP
email: info@iconbooks.net
www.introducingbooks.com

Sold in the UK, Europe and Asia
by Faber & Faber Ltd,
Bloomsbury House,
74–77 Great Russell Street,
London WC1B 3DA or their agents

Distributed in South Africa
by Jonathan Ball,
Office B4, The District,
41 Sir Lowry Road,
Woodstock 7925

Distributed in Australia and
New Zealand by Allen & Unwin Pty Ltd
PO Box 8500, 83 Alexander Street,
Crows Nest, NSW 2065

Distributed to the trade in the USA
by Consortium Book Sales
and Distribution, The Keg House,
34 Thirteenth Avenue NE, Suite 101,
Minneapolis, MN 55413-1007

Distributed in Canada
by Penguin Books Canada,
90 Eglinton Avenue East,
Suite 700, Toronto,
Ontario M4P 2Y3

Previous edition published in the UK
and Australia in 1999

ISBN: 978-184831-182-4

Text and illustrations copyright © 2012 Icon Books Ltd

Originating editor: Richard Appignanesi

Printed and bound in the UK by Clays Ltd, St Ives plc

What is Evolutionary Psychology?

Evolutionary psychology is the combination of two sciences – **evolutionary biology** and **cognitive psychology**. These two sciences are like two pieces of a jigsaw puzzle. We need both pieces if we want to understand human behaviour.

We will begin by looking at each of these sciences separately. Then we will see how evolutionary psychology puts them together to arrive at a complete scientific account of human nature.

Cognitive Psychology

Cognitive psychology is the most powerful theory of the mind ever developed. It has transformed psychology from a vague set of unclear ideas into a true science. There are two main ideas.

(1)
Actions are caused by mental processes.

(2)
The mind is a computer.

Let's have a look at these two ideas in more detail.

Actions Are Caused by Mental Processes

Psychology is the science of human behaviour. It attempts to explain why humans act the way they do.

We are all amateur psychologists. We constantly offer explanations for our actions and for the actions of others. For example, when I see Jim pick up an umbrella as he leaves the house, I might explain this action in the following way.

JIM THINKS IT'S GOING TO RAIN, AND HE WANTS TO STAY DRY.

THIS KIND OF EXPLANATION IS CALLED A MENTALISTIC EXPLANATION BECAUSE IT REFERS TO MENTAL PROCESSES LIKE BELIEFS AND DESIRES.

When we say that "Jim *thought* it was going to rain", we are saying that Jim had a certain *belief*. When we say that "Jim *wanted* to stay dry", we are saying that Jim had a certain *desire*.

Behaviourist Psychology

When we explain actions by referring to beliefs and desires, we are claiming that these mental processes are the *causes* of our actions. This way of explaining actions in terms of beliefs and desires is so common that philosophers call it "commonsense psychology" or "folk psychology". Folk psychology has been around for thousands of years.

In the 1920s, some psychologists claimed that folk psychology was unscientific. **J.B. Watson** (1878-1958) and **B.F. Skinner** (1904-90) argued that beliefs, desires and other mental processes were not real things. They thought that the only way for psychology to become a true science was to give up talking about such "mythical entities".

This view is known as Behaviourism. From the 1920s until the 1960s, most psychologists were Behaviourists. During these years, most psychologists denied the existence of "the mind".

6

In the 1960s, psychologists began to reject behaviourism. There were two main reasons for this. On the one hand, as a purely logical matter, philosophers realized that they simply could not eliminate talk about beliefs and desires from explanations of human behaviour. On the other hand, the development of computers, and work in artificial intelligence, provided a way of testing – and refuting – Behaviourist theories of learning.

With the abandonment of Behaviourism, it once again became acceptable for scientists to talk about "the mind".

THE MIND IS A VALID SCIENTIFIC CONCEPT AFTER ALL.

THIS IS THE FIRST MAIN IDEA OF COGNITIVE PSYCHOLOGY.

In this sense, cognitive psychology has a lot in common with folk psychology. Like folk psychology, cognitive psychology explains actions by referring to mental processes. Unlike folk psychology, however, cognitive psychology has a very precise idea of what these mental processes are – they are *computations*. This takes us on to the second main idea of cognitive psychology.

The Mind is a Computer

The second main idea of cognitive psychology is that the mind is a computer program. But cognitive psychologists mean something very special by the term "computer". Basing themselves on the pioneering work of the British mathematician **Alan Turing** (1912-54), cognitive psychologists define a computer as a set of operations for processing information.

IN OTHE WORDS, A COMPUTER IS NOT A PHYSICAL MACHINE, BUT RATHER AN ABSTRACT SPECIFICATION OF A POSSIBLE MACHINE.

A COMPUTER, IN THIS SENSE, MAY BE BUILT IN MANY DIFFERENT WAYS.

Many different sorts of physical machine could process information in the same way. In this case, even though the machines would have physically different designs, they would all be the same kind of computer.

So, a computer is not a piece of hardware, but a piece of software. The essence of a computer does not lie in the materials from which it is made, but in the programs it executes. In order to run a program, such as a computer game, you need a machine to run it on. But you can run the same program on different kinds of machine.

THE MACHINES ARE PHYSICALLY DIFFERENT, BUT WHEN YOU INSTALL THE SAME PROGRAM ON THEM, THEY BEHAVE IN THE SAME WAY.

THE KEY TO THE BEHAVIOUR IS THE PROGRAM, NOT THE MATERIALS OUT OF WHICH THE MACHINE IS MADE.

For cognitive psychology, then, the mind is a piece of **software**. It is a very complicated kind of program. Cognitive psychologists can describe this program in the language of information-processing without needing to describe the details of the brain. The brain is just the physical machine that runs the program called the mind. The brain is the hardware, the mind is the software.

Metaphors of the Mind

People have often attempted to understand the mind by comparing it with the latest technology. In the past few hundred years, the mind has been described as a clock, a watch, a telegraph system, and much else. In the late 19th century, **Sigmund Freud** (1856-1939) borrowed from contemporary developments in hydraulics, and compared the mind to a system of channels and waterways.

THE WATERWAYS COULD SOMETIMES BE BLOCKED, IN WHICH CASE THE FLUID WOULD SOON OVERFLOW INTO ANOTHER CHANNEL.

The problem with all these comparisons was that they were little more than interesting metaphors. They did not help very much to advance understanding of the mind because there was no clear way of generating testable predictions from them.

A Testable Model

All this changed with the advent of cognitive psychology. Comparing the mind to a computer was different from previous technological analogies because the precise language of information-processing allowed **testable hypotheses** about the mind to be clearly formulated.

Also, there is a much better reason for comparing the mind to a computer than to a clock or an irrigation system – they have the same function.

THE FUNCTION OF THE MIND, LIKE THAT OF THE COMPUTER, IS TO PROCESS INFORMATION.

IT IS NOT TO TELL THE TIME OR TO DISTRIBUTE WATER.

Unlike earlier comparisons, then, the computational theory of mind can be taken literally; the mind is not just *like* a computer, it *is* a computer.

This concludes our brief overview of cognitive science. It is now time to examine the other piece of the jigsaw puzzle: **evolutionary biology**.

Evolutionary Biology

During the last two thousand years, most people in the West believed that human beings had been created directly by God. According to the Bible, the first two human beings, Adam and Eve, had no father or mother, and sprang into existence in adult form. In the 18th and early 19th centuries, some people began to question this view, including **Erasmus Darwin** (1731-1802), grandfather of Charles.

I WROTE A POEM ABOUT EVOLUTION BEFORE CHARLES WAS EVEN BORN.

THE ORIGIN OF SPECIES CHARLES DARWIN 1859

But it wasn't until **Charles Darwin** (1809--82) published *The Origin of Species* in 1859 that the sceptics had an alternative explanation for the origin of humanity. This alternative is evolutionary biology.

According to evolutionary biology, human beings are descended from ape-like ancestors and ultimately share a single common ancestor with all other living things on earth. This common ancestor, the first living thing, lived about 4 billion years ago. It was very simple.

IN FACT, IT WAS FAR LESS COMPLEX THAN A SINGLE CELL.

About 3.5 billion years ago, some of these little creatures began to gang up together and form the first cells. Around 600 million years ago, the first multicellular organisms began to appear: small worms and other sea-dwelling creatures.

A hundred million years later, the first land-dwelling organisms appeared – first microbes, then plants. This paved the way for terrestrial animals, including insects, and then amphibians. From amphibians came reptiles, birds and mammals. The first primates appeared around 55 million years ago.

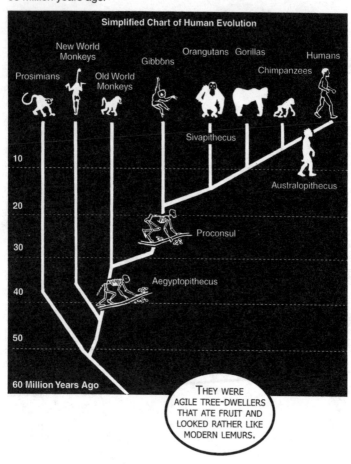

From these creatures are descended monkeys, apes and humans.
The first true humans (*Homo sapiens sapiens*) appeared about 150,000 years ago in Africa.

Heredity and Mutation

How did all of this come about? What is it that drives evolution? There is no mysterious deity guiding the process. It all happens because of two things: **heredity** and **mutation**.

HEREDITY MEANS THAT OFFSPRING TEND TO RESEMBLE THEIR PARENTS.

HEREDITY

MUTATION MEANS THAT SOMETIMES THIS RESEMBLANCE IS NOT PERFECT.

MUTATION

In order to understand both of these things, we must understand something about *genes*.

Genes

Every cell in every organism contains a full set of instructions for making a copy of that organism. These instructions are called "genes" and are written not in ink but in a molecule called DNA. We can imagine genes as little beads threaded along a long string inside each cell. Each bead is an instruction (or a group of instructions) that says something like: brown hair, blue eyes, short temper, etc.

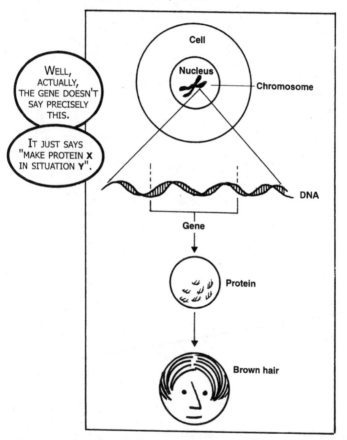

However, since one result of making protein x in environment y is that you end up with brown hair, or blue eyes, or a short temper, it's fine to say that the gene is an instruction for brown hair, blue eyes, etc.

Heredity

The reason why offspring tend to resemble their parents is that they inherit their genes from their parents. An elephant baby looks like an elephant, not like a panda, because the elephant baby inherits elephant genes from its parents. We can think of all the different elephant genes as existing in a separate pool from panda genes.

EACH ELEPHANT IS MADE FROM A SET OF GENES DRAWN FROM THE ELEPHANT GENE POOL.

EACH PANDA IS MADE FROM A SET OF GENES FROM THE PANDA GENE POOL.

In the elephant gene pool, there are genes that influence the size of the elephant, genes that influence the length of its trunk, etc. And the reason tall elephants generally have tall children is that they pass genes for tallness on to their children.

Mutation

But what about mutation? Why do offspring sometimes look different from their parents? This may happen because sometimes, a gene inside one cell just happens to change. For example, a gene that normally makes people taller than average might change into a gene that makes people grow an extra finger (unlikely, but not impossible). A new gene has been born!

WE CALL THE BIRTH OF A NEW GENE A "MUTATION".

THIS DOESN'T MEAN IT'S NECESSARILY BAD. BIOLOGISTS USE THE WORD IN A NEUTRAL WAY.

As a matter of fact, however, most mutations are harmful. Only a few mutations turn out to be beneficial, in the sense of increasing your chances of surviving and reproducing.

When a mutant gene arises, it is the only one of its kind in the gene pool. If its effect is to decrease one's chances of surviving and reproducing, then it probably won't get passed on to any offspring. In other words, it won't last long in the gene pool. On the other hand, if it increases your chances of surviving and reproducing, it will get passed on to more offspring, who will pass it on to even more offspring, and eventually there will be lots of copies of the gene in the gene pool.

In this way, each gene pool gradually changes over time. One by one, mutant genes arise and spread through the gene pool. After many generations, the gene pool is filled with lots of new genes. The bodies built by these genes look very different from the bodies built by the genes that once filled the gene pool. A new species has evolved.

Adaptation and Natural Selection

We have just seen how the evolution of life on earth is driven by two processes: heredity and mutation. These two processes are enough to explain how a single living thing that existed 4 billion years ago gave rise to the thousands of different species we see on the earth today. However, evolutionary biologists are not just interested in the diversity of species; they are also interested in the particular characteristics that distinguish each species, many of which give the appearance of having been "designed" for a particular purpose.

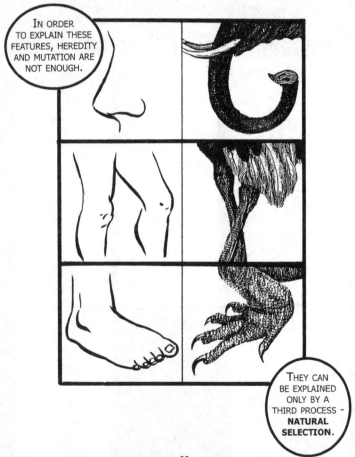

The classic example of a characteristic that seems to have been "designed" for a particular purpose is the eye. The eye seems to have been designed for seeing. Like a camera, it has a focusing lens and a light-sensitive screen positioned just at the focal plane of the lens. It has a transparent cornea that protects the lens, and an iris that gets bigger and smaller to let in just the right amount of light. All these things make sense only when we realize that they are part of a complex machine designed for seeing.

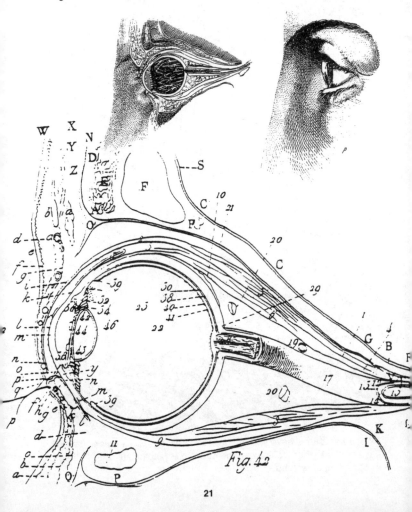

Fig. 42

Useful Design

The same can be said of many other parts of animals and plants.

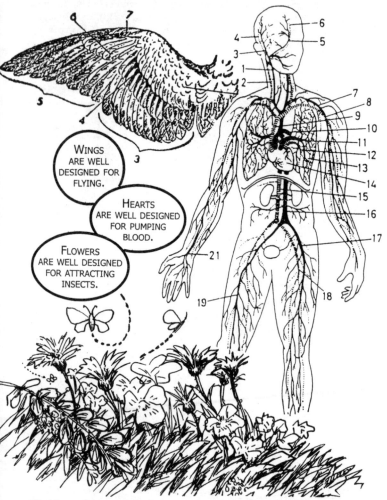

All of these things have features that a knowledgeable engineer might have built into them to achieve their purposes. Biologists refer to these things as **adaptations**.

22

The Argument from Design

For hundreds of years, people in the West thought that adaptations were an irrefutable proof of the existence of God. The most famous exponent of this view was the English theologian **William Paley** (1743-1805). In his book, *Natural Theology* (1802), he compared adaptations like eyes or wings to complex machines designed by humans, such as clocks and watches.

IF YOU FOUND A WATCH LYING ON THE GROUND, YOU WOULDN'T THINK IT HAD JUST APPEARED BY CHANCE.

YOU WOULD NATURALLY INFER THAT IT HAD BEEN MADE BY AN INTELLIGENT DESIGNER.

And just as a watch implies the existence of a watchmaker, Paley claimed, the eye implies the existence of an eyemaker – God.

Not by Coincidence...

Paley was right about one thing. Complex machines like watches and eyes are extremely improbable arrangements of matter. To claim that they could have come into existence in one single cosmic coincidence would be ludicrous. That would be about as likely as a hurricane blowing through a junkyard and assembling a Boeing 747 out of the scrap metal.

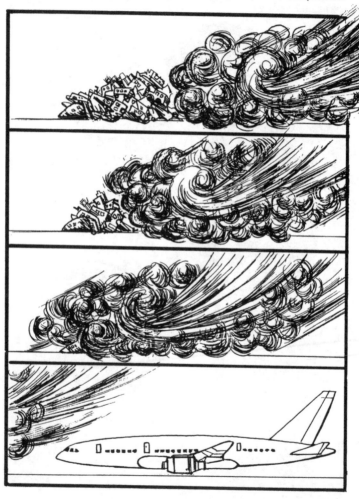

Natura non facit saltum

But Paley was wrong in thinking that the only alternative to such a ludicrous scenario was that eyes and other adaptations had been designed by God. Darwin's theory of natural selection provides another alternative. Darwin argued that complex machines like the eye could evolve by a completely natural process, without the aid of any supernatural being.

IT EVOLVES BY ACCUMULATING **MANY SMALL CHANGES** OVER A LONG PERIOD OF TIME.

LONG BEFORE DARWIN, I POINTED OUT THAT NATURE DOES NOT MAKE LEAPS ... **NON FACIT SALTUM.**

PHILOSOPHIA BOTANICA
CAROLUS LINNAEUS 1751

CAROLUS LINNAEUS (1707-78)

25

Improvement by Accident

This is how evolutionary biology explains the evolution of complex designs like the eye. Adaptations do not come about all in one go, by a single large mutation, but evolve gradually by accumulating hundreds of very small mutations. The mutations occur at random, with no plan in mind.

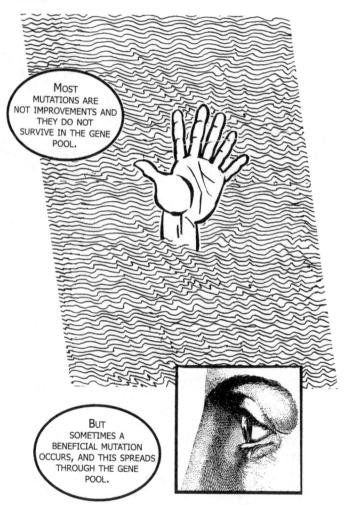

The Evolution of the Eye

In the case of the eye, for example, the first small change was probably a slight increase in the sensitivity to light of a small piece of skin. All skin is slightly sensitive to light anyway, and it is not difficult to imagine that the offspring of one of our eyeless ancestors happened to be born with a bit of skin slightly more sensitive to light than normal. This was just an accident, of course.

It also just happened that this particular accident was a lucky accident, because it allowed the mutant baby to detect the shadow of a predator more quickly, and thus escape faster than its eyeless parents and siblings could do.

Of course, there were many other accidents that weren't quite so lucky – many other mutant babies whose unusual features were disadvantageous rather than beneficial. These mutants did not have any offspring.

But the lucky mutant was more successful and had lots of offspring. Moreover, it passed the new gene for light-sensitive skin-bits on to its offspring, so the new gene spread through the population and eventually everyone had the light-sensitive skin patches. Later on, there were other mutations, some of which were also beneficial. The light-sensitive skin patches became light-sensitive concave dips, which were then filled in with transparent fluid and finally covered over with a lens. The eye had evolved by a process of natural selection.

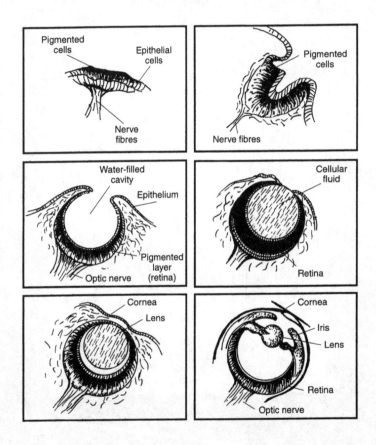

The Blind Watchmaker

Natural selection, then, builds adaptations by accumulating many small accidental changes. The British biologist **Richard Dawkins** (b. 1941) has compared natural selection to a "blind watchmaker". It is a watchmaker because it produces complex designs, but it is blind because it doesn't produce these designs by conscious foresight, but simply by accumulating a series of random accidents.

This concludes our brief survey of evolutionary biology. Now it is time to fit the two pieces of the jigsaw puzzle together.

Fitting the Pieces of the Jigsaw Puzzle Together

Evolutionary psychology is the combination of cognitive psychology and evolutionary biology. But why should we combine these two sciences? What have they got to do with each other? The answer is simple.

COGNITIVE PSYCHOLOGY TELLS US THAT THE MIND EXHIBITS A VERY COMPLEX DESIGN.

EVOLUTIONARY BIOLOGY TELLS US THAT COMPLEX DESIGNS IN NATURE CAN ONLY COME ABOUT BY NATURAL SELECTION.

THEREFORE, THE DESIGN OF THE MIND MUST HAVE EVOLVED BY A PROCESS OF NATURAL SELECTION.

What is meant by saying that the mind is a "complex design"? Just how complex is the mind?

General-Purpose Problem-Solver?

When cognitive psychologists first began to investigate the mind, they thought that it would be a very simple kind of program.

When they set out to test this hypothesis, however, the cognitive psychologists found that they were wrong. They wrote some very simple programs that could solve very abstract problems, but they found that these programs were unable to do many of the things that humans do easily.

Learning a Language

One of these things that humans do easily is learning a language. In the late 1950s, the American linguist **Noam Chomsky** (b. 1928) showed that a general-purpose learning program simply could not learn a language under the same conditions as normal human children.

IN ORDER FOR CHILDREN TO LEARN A LANGUAGE, THEY MUST FIRST HEAR ADULTS SPEAKING IT.

HOW'S YOU THEN? YOU TIRED? ... ER ... TIME FOR BEDDY-BYES.

BUT ADULT SPEECH CONTAINS LOTS OF ERRORS, AND NO INDICATION OF WHAT IS CORRECT AND INCORRECT.

The technical term for this faulty data is "the poverty of the stimulus". Learning a language based on this information alone would be like trying to figure out the rules of chess just by observing a few chess games in which some of the moves were illegal (but without knowing *which* moves were illegal). This would be impossible unless you already knew what information to look for.

Language Acquisition

So the only program that could learn a human language is a specific one that has been pre-programmed with specific information relevant just to language learning. Chomsky concluded that there is an innate "language acquisition device" (LAD) in the mind which knows what kinds of rules human languages can have. Human languages have a limited number of structures, which are collectively known as "Universal Grammar".

WHEN A CHILD LEARNS ITS FIRST LANGUAGE, HE OR SHE DOESN'T START FROM SCRATCH.

THEY SIMPLY SELECT FROM THEIR INNATE KNOWLEDGE OF UNIVERSAL GRAMMAR THE RULES THAT THEY HEAR BEING USED AROUND THEM.

In a sense, language isn't something that is *learned*; it is more appropriate to say that it just *develops* naturally, like a biological organ or an instinct.

Vision

Chomsky's pioneering work on language was followed by similar discoveries in other areas of psychology. **David Marr** (1945-80) showed how another apparently simple task – seeing – was also very complex. Writing a program that could enable a robot to recognize even simple objects proved incredibly difficult.

David Marr's theory of vision: we reconstruct three-dimensional images by building them up from simpler shapes like cylinders.

Modularity

Cognitive psychologists began to realize that the mind was far more complex than they had first imagined. In 1983, the American philosopher and psychologist **Jerry Fodor** (b. 1935) reached a stunning conclusion.

THE MIND COULD NOT POSSIBLY BE A SINGLE, GENERAL-PURPOSE PROGRAM.

INSTEAD, IT HAS TO BE A COLLECTION OF MANY SPECIAL-PURPOSE PROGRAMS, EACH WITH ITS OWN RULES.

TASTE MODULE

SOUND MODULE

LANGUAGE MODULE

CENTRAL PROCESSES

VISION MODULE

TOUCH MODULE

SMELL MODULE

Fodor called these special-purpose programs "modules".

The modular theory of mind is still quite new, and is not yet accepted by all cognitive psychologists, but it is becoming more influential. Although it is a very new idea, in a way it is also a return to a very old idea. For hundreds of years, people have divided the mind into "faculties". In the 19th century, **Franz Joseph Gall** (1758-1828) divided the mind into dozens of distinct capacities.

JUST AS THE OLDER UNIVERSITIES WERE DIVIDED INTO DIFFERENT "FACULTIES" ...

Faculty psychology was largely abandoned at the beginning of the 20th century, but now, with the modular theory of mind, it is regaining prominence.

Massive Modularity

John Tooby and **Leda Cosmides**, two American psychologists who have pioneered many developments in evolutionary psychology, argue that there are hundreds, perhaps even thousands, of these special-purpose modules in the human mind.

This view is sometimes called the "massive modularity" thesis to distinguish it from a more limited view of modularity.

When Fodor proposed a return to the tradition of "faculty psychology" in his 1983 book, *The Modularity of Mind*, he didn't envisage hundreds of modules. He proposed that there were only a few of them. There were modules for processing sensory input (vision, sound, taste, touch, smell and language), but no more. Fodor claimed that these "input systems" fed information into general-purpose programs called "central processes". The central processes were not modular in Fodor's account. Fodor thinks evolutionary psychology has gone too far.

THIS IS MODULARITY GONE MAD!

No Central Processes

Evolutionary psychologists are opposed to Fodor's idea of "general-purpose central processes" for the same reason as they are opposed to the idea that the whole mind is a general-purpose program.

Modules and Adaptations

A modular mind is clearly far more complex than a single general-purpose program. It has lots of interlocking parts that function smoothly together to process information. It has an innate structure that develops naturally, like a biological organ. According to evolutionary biology, these characteristics occur only as a result of natural selection.

WE CAN THEREFORE ASK HOW THE DIFFERENT BITS OF THE MIND EVOLVED.

EVOLUTIONARY PSYCHOLOGY IS THE RESEARCH PROGRAM THAT ATTEMPTS TO ANSWER THIS QUESTION.

Adaptations and Environments

According to evolutionary psychology, the various mental modules are adaptations designed by natural selection. Every adaptation is designed to solve an adaptive problem. An adaptive problem is something that an organism needs to solve in order to survive and reproduce.

FOR EXAMPLE, ONE IMPORTANT ADAPTIVE PROBLEM FACED BY MANY ANIMALS IS THE PROBLEM OF STAYING WARM.

SOME ANIMALS SOLVE THIS PROBLEM BY DEVELOPING COATS OF FUR.

OTHERS SOLVE IT BY THICK LAYERS OF BLUBBER.

Evolving Modules

Different environments pose different adaptive problems and so require different adaptations. There is not much point in having eyes if you live deep underground, where there is no light. If you want to understand any adaptation, therefore, you must know something about the environment in which it evolved.

What was the environment in which the various modules in the human mind evolved? This is a tricky question, because the modules did not all evolve at the same time, so they did not all evolve in the same environment.

Some modules evolved relatively recently, after the human species split from that of our closest relative, the chimpanzee. These modules are unique to humans.

Simplified Chart of Human Evolution

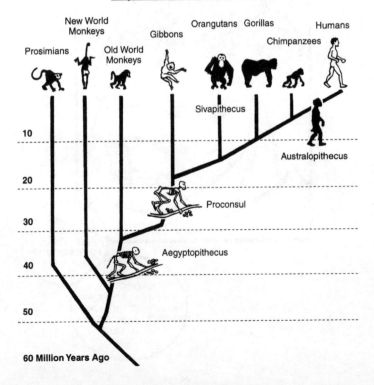

Shared and Unique Modules

Other modules evolved a long time ago, when the common ancestor of humans and reptiles was alive. These modules are not unique to humans. There are similar modules in the minds of reptiles. This does not mean that we have a "reptilian" bit in our mind, however. Mental modules, like all adaptations, do not stop evolving once they have appeared. They keep changing along with the environment. So, for example, both humans and crocodiles have eyes because they are descended from the same ancestral species in which eyes first evolved. But this does not mean that humans have reptilian eyes.

HUMANS AND CROCODILES HAVE SLIGHTLY DIFFERENT KINDS OF EYE.

BECAUSE OUR EYES HAVE EVOLVED IN DIFFERENT WAYS SINCE THE HUMAN LINEAGE DIVERGED FROM THE REPTILIAN LINEAGE.

If we want to investigate the most distinctively human modules, the ones we don't share with any other animals, we will have to look at the environment in which our ancestors lived after the human lineage split from that of the chimpanzee.

Out of Africa

Around 100,000 years ago, some of our ancestors began to emigrate out of Africa, and eventually colonized the whole world. But 100,000 years is only about 5,000 generations – too short a time for evolution to produce any major changes. Humans haven't changed much in that time, so we can ignore it when discussing the evolution of the mind. This means that all the history of human civilization and culture, from the birth of agriculture some 10,000 years ago until the present, is irrelevant to understanding the design of the human mind.

OUR MINDS DID NOT EVOLVE IN A WORLD OF CITIES AND CARS, NOR EVEN IN A WORLD OF PLOUGHS AND FARMING.

WE ARE ALL "STONE-AGERS LIVING IN THE FAST LANE".

The Social Environment

What was life like on the African savannahs? The climate was hot and sunny, and the flat plains were covered in long grass dotted with trees, some of which were rich in high-quality food like fruit and nuts. This was the *physical* environment in which the human mind evolved. However, when we are considering the evolution of the human mind, it is just as important – perhaps even more important – to consider the *social* environment.

Like most primates, our ancestors lived in tightly-knit groups with a complex social structure. Interacting with the other people in the group was just as important for their survival as being able to detect and escape from predators.

Adaptive Problems

Now that we know a little bit about the environment in which our most recent ancestors lived, we can ask what adaptive problems they faced. When we know what adaptive problems they faced, we can make some educated guesses about the kinds of mental adaptations (mental modules) that natural selection might have produced to solve them. Then, as with any other science, we can try to find evidence to see whether these guesses are right or wrong.

SELECTING MATES.

COMMUNICATING WITH OTHER PEOPLE.

So what were the adaptive problems faced by our hominid ancestors? Various considerations drawn from biology, primatology, archaeology and anthropology suggest what the most important adaptive problems would have been.

AVOIDING PREDATORS.

EATING THE RIGHT FOOD.

FORMING ALLIANCES AND FRIENDSHIPS.

PROVIDING HELP TO CHILDREN AND OTHER RELATIVES.

READING OTHER PEOPLE'S MINDS.

All of these things are crucial for passing on your genes. So we should expect natural selection to have designed mental modules that enabled our ancestors to achieve these objectives in the ancestral environment. In the next part of this book we will examine these modules in more detail, beginning with predator avoidance.

Predator-Avoidance Modules

Avoiding predators is a very important problem from the genes' point of view. Genes cannot get themselves passed on to the next generation if their owner is eaten. Any genes that tend to make their owners avoid predators will therefore spread throughout the population.

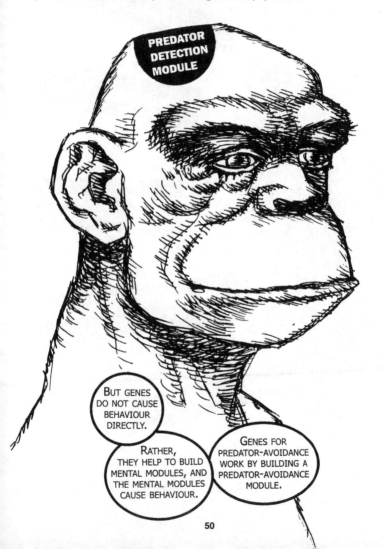

What would a predator-avoidance module look like? It would have to be able to detect possible predators, distinguish those that were real dangers from those that weren't, and – in the case of real dangers – trigger avoidant or defensive behaviours.

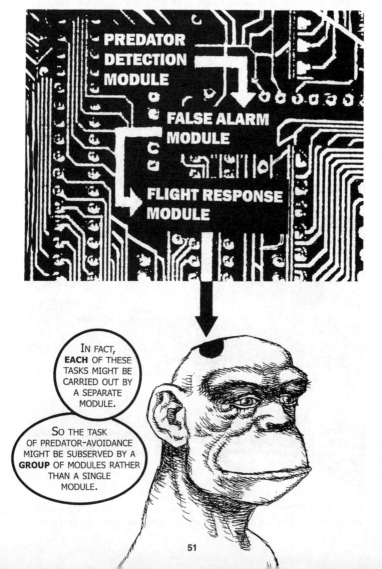

PREDATOR
DETECTION
MODULE

FALSE ALARM
MODULE

FLIGHT RESPONSE
MODULE

IN FACT, **EACH** OF THESE TASKS MIGHT BE CARRIED OUT BY A SEPARATE MODULE.

SO THE TASK OF PREDATOR-AVOIDANCE MIGHT BE SUBSERVED BY A **GROUP** OF MODULES RATHER THAN A SINGLE MODULE.

Detecting Predators

The first module in the predator-avoidance system would detect possible predators. With any detection system, however, there is a trade-off between accuracy and speed. Think of a burglar alarm. On the one hand, you want the alarm to be accurate – you don't want it to be triggered by stray cats. You don't want false alarms. On the other hand, you also want an alarm that goes off immediately a burglar attempts to break in. It's not much use having a burglar alarm that rings five minutes after the burglar has left the house.

The more accurate the alarm is, the slower it is. Conversely, if you want a faster alarm, you will have to put up with a higher rate of false alarms.

Which is more costly – a false alarm or a slow detector? If it is a question of detecting predators, a false alarm causes you to waste energy by running away from something that is not in fact a danger. A slow detector, however, can cause you to be eaten. So it is better to have a fast system that occasionally gives false alarms than a slow system that is always accurate. So we should expect the predator-detection module to be fast and inaccurate rather than slow and precise.

False Alarms

While you are reacting to the alarm given off by the predator-detection module, another module can then take a bit more time to decide whether or not the alarm was triggered by a genuine danger. If it was, then the avoidance behaviours are maintained. If the second module decides that the first module gave a false alarm, however, it can override the avoidance behaviour.

Two Neural Pathways

There is some evidence that this is in fact the case. The American neuroscientist **Joseph LeDoux** has shown that the emotion of fear – which prepares us to flee from predators or *freeze* to avoid being seen – is subserved by *two* neural mechanisms. One "fast and dirty" mechanism is, as the name suggests, very quick but not very accurate. It often gives false alarms. The other mechanism is much more accurate but slower.

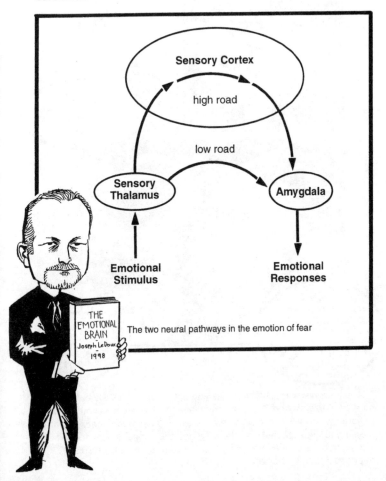

The two neural pathways in the emotion of fear

The fast and dirty mechanism gets you out of trouble quickly but gives off some false alarms. The slow and clean mechanism tells you when the alarms are false, and so stops you wasting too much energy in reacting to them. Sometimes the slow and clean mechanism doesn't kick in, and we continue reacting to false alarms. This may be what happens in some phobias.

Food Preference Modules

Genes that predisposed their owners to consume nutritious food and avoid poisonous food would spread through the population. As with predator-avoidance, however, genes do not cause this behaviour directly. They build mental mechanisms that lead us to desire some foods and dislike others.

Fat and Sugar

Animal fat and sugar are highly nutritious, but they were relatively scarce in the African savannah where our ancestors lived. To get animal fat it was necessary to kill an animal or scavenge one that had already been killed. To get sugar it was necessary to find ripe fruit. Both of these were complicated – and sometimes dangerous – tasks. In a situation like this, it would have been highly adaptive to have strong desires for fat and sugar.

On balance, they would tend to consume more of these nutritious foods, and so they would be more likely to pass on their genes – including their genes for liking fat and sugar.

Environmental Mismatch

Fat and sugar are bad for you if you eat too much of them, but in ancestral environments these resources were scarce, so there wasn't much chance of consuming too much. Today, however, we have supermarkets and fast-food restaurants to cater for our evolved tastes. Fat and sugar are no longer difficult to find.

We were designed to live in such a different environment, and this "environmental mismatch" is the source of many current problems.

Disgust

Eating the right food does not just involve seeking out nutritious food. It is also important to avoid poisonous food. Just as natural selection has designed modules that make us prefer fat and sugar, so it has also designed modules that make us avoid eating rotting flesh and faeces.

In other words, when the module detects a food that it thinks is poisonous, it activates the feeling of disgust, and it is this feeling – not any conscious deliberation – that makes us avoid the food.

Alliance-Formation Modules

The two adaptive problems we have just examined – avoiding predators and eating the right food – are problems posed by the physical environment. However, as we have already seen, when considering the evolution of the mind, it is just as important to consider the problems posed by the social environment.

The social environment refers to the other conspecifics (animals of the same species) with whom you live. For many animals, the social environment is virtually non-existent, because they live solitary lives.

Living in Groups

Primates are unusual in that they live in tightly-knit social groups with complex hierarchies and alliances.

LIVING IN GROUPS BENEFITS PRIMATES BECAUSE IT PROVIDES EXTRA DEFENCES AGAINST PREDATORS.

It is harder for a predator to catch an animal in a group than an isolated animal because groups have more eyes to detect predators, and because other group members can come to the aid of one who is being attacked.

Alliances and Coalitions

But group living also poses adaptive problems for primates. With lots of other conspecifics around you, all with the same food preferences, competition becomes more intense. Squabbles for scarce resources become common.

Increasing the Group

Our ancestors continued and extended this primate lifestyle. After the human lineage split from the chimpanzee lineage some six million years ago, the size of human groups began to increase.

THE INCREASE IN GROUP-SIZE MEANT THAT FORMING ALLIANCES BECAME EVEN MORE IMPORTANT FOR SURVIVAL.

For our ancestors, forming alliances and friendships was just as vital as eating the right food. Those who lacked the ability to form alliances and friendships were in as much danger as those who lacked the ability to detect predators.

Reciprocal Altruism

But forming alliances is not an easy task. The main problem is the risk of defection. An alliance is an "I'll help you if you help me" arrangement. It is all about exchanging favours – which biologists call "reciprocal altruism". But there is a problem with any such arrangement.

This is known as the "free-rider" problem and it is the fundamental adaptive problem posed by group living.

The Free-Rider Problem

Those animals that cannot solve the free-rider problem cannot live in groups. To see why, imagine a group of animals that strikes up an alliance in which one of the members is a free-rider. Whenever the free-rider is in danger, or hungry, the other members of the alliance come to his aid. The other members pay a cost for helping the free-rider, by risking their lives for him or by giving him some of their precious food. The free-rider enjoys these benefits, but never pays the costs of returning the favours.

UNDETECTED, THE FREE-RIDER WILL OBVIOUSLY BE MORE SUCCESSFUL AT SURVIVING AND REPRODUCING THAN THE PUBLIC-SPIRITED SUCKERS.

SO GENES FOR FREE-RIDING WILL BECOME MORE FREQUENT IN THE GENE POOL.

EVENTUALLY, EVERYONE WILL BE A FREE-RIDER.

But then, no one will be helping anyone else. Alliances will disintegrate and group-living will no longer be possible.

The Evolution of Cooperation

All animals that live in groups have found ways of solving the free-rider problem. Different species solve the problem in different ways, but there are some fundamental conditions that any solution must meet. These conditions were worked out by an American political scientist called **Robert Axelrod** in the early 1980s. Axelrod showed that the free-rider problem can only be solved if the following three conditions are satisfied.

3. Organisms can remember how those they have met before have treated them on previous encounters.

1. Organisms encounter the same organisms repeatedly.

2. Organisms can recognise those they have met before and distinguish them from strangers.

I DISCOVERED THESE THREE CONDITIONS BY ORGANIZING A **TOURNAMENT** IN WHICH DIFFERENT COMPUTER PROGRAMS COMPETED AGAINST EACH OTHER.

Tit-for-Tat

Why are Axelrod's three conditions necessary for solving the free-rider problem? The answer has to do with punishment and reward. When these three conditions are satisfied, free-riders can be punished and cooperators can be rewarded. Free-riders who have refused to do return favours can be punished by refusing to do any more favours for them. Cooperators can be rewarded by continuing to help them when they need it.

This simple strategy is called "tit-for-tat". When a group of organisms interact on the basis of tit-for-tat, free-riders no longer have the advantage. Cooperation can evolve and group cohesion can be maintained.

All three conditions for using tit-for-tat were present in our hominid ancestors. In the small, tightly-knit groups of fifty to a hundred people in which they lived, the first condition was easily satisfied. Day after day, we interact with the same people. The second condition is satisfied by the evolution of a sophisticated face-recognition module. The third condition is met by the evolution of a sophisticated memory for recording social interaction.

For each acquaintance, we keep a mental tally of how much they have done for us and how much we have done for them. If the tally shows that someone has consistently done less for us than we have done for them, then the next time they ask for help, we will be less inclined to give it. We punish free-riding by refusing to cooperate.

Cognitive Adaptations for Social Exchange

IN ORDER TO KEEP A MENTAL TALLY, WE MUST HAVE SOME WAY OF WORKING OUT THE VALUE OF THE FAVOURS THAT OTHERS DO FOR US.

THERE MUST BE SOME WAY OF COMPARING THIS WITH THE VALUE OF THE FAVOURS THAT WE DO FOR OTHERS.

Leda Cosmides and John Tooby have argued that humans evolved special modules for calculating these things. They propose that these cognitive adaptations are the basis of all human behaviour involving exchange – from trading favours to trading stocks and shares.

The calculations performed by these "social accounting" modules must take into account a whole range of variables when working out the value of a favour. The value of a favour depends both on the cost to the donor and the benefit to the recipient. A favour that costs the donor a lot is worth more than a favour that costs the donor little. A favour that benefits the recipient a lot is worth more than a favour that benefits the recipient a little. The value of a favour is the ratio between the cost to the donor and benefit to the recipient.

The costs and benefits of any kind of favour are not fixed in advance, but depend on the context.

The social accounting modules must consider all these details.

Modules for Helping Children and Other Relatives

All this talk about social accounting and tit-for-tat suggests that altruism and cooperation can only evolve on a strictly reciprocal basis. If this were true, no animal would ever help another animal unless there was a good chance of receiving an equally valuable favour in return. But this is clearly not the case.

NATURE IS FULL OF EXAMPLES OF ANIMALS THAT PROVIDE HELP TO OTHER ANIMALS FROM WHOM THEY CANNOT EXPECT ANY REPAYMENT.

AND HUMANS ARE NO EXCEPTION.

Parenting is the most obvious example of such non-reciprocal altruism. In all species that care for their young, parents provide help that they never expect their offspring to repay. Humans provide more intensive and long-lasting care for their offspring than any other species, and this is entirely non-reciprocal. So there must be another element that enters into the social-cooperation modules besides the social accounting already described. What is it?

Kin Selection

The example of parenting provides a clue to what this element is. When biologists examined the examples of non-reciprocal altruism in the animal kingdom, they noticed that they all had one feature in common. This kind of altruism is directed exclusively towards genetic relatives. In 1964, the British biologist **William Hamilton** came up with a theory to explain why this was the case. He argued that the fundamental unit of evolution was not the organism but the individual gene.

Non-reciprocal altruism at the level of the organism, such as the care that parents provide for their children, is the result of "selfishness" at the level of the gene. In 1975, the British biologist **Richard Dawkins** popularized Hamilton's ideas in his famous book, *The Selfish Gene*.

How Related Are You?

Hamilton showed that non-reciprocal altruism could evolve whenever organisms had some means of estimating their "degree of relatedness" to other organisms. The degree of relatedness is the chance that a randomly chosen gene in one organism will be shared by another organism as a result of common descent. The British geneticist **Sewall Wright** (1889-1988) had already coined the symbol *r* in 1922 for this concept which he called the "coefficient of relatedness".

I CALCULATED THE FOLLOWING VALUES FOR *r*.

Type of relative	Examples	Value of *r*
First-degree relatives	Parents, children, full siblings	50%
Second-degree relatives	Grandparents, grandchildren, half siblings, uncles, aunts, nephews, nieces	25%
Third-degree relatives	First cousins	12.5%

Hamilton's Rule

Hamilton showed that non-reciprocal altruism can evolve whenever there are mechanisms that ensure that the coefficient of relatedness will tend to exceed the cost-benefit ratio of the altruistic act. This can be written as the following equation.

The Evolution of Nepotism

What mental mechanisms evolved to help our ancestors follow Hamilton's rule? Clearly, they must have had some mechanism for distinguishing kin from non-kin, and assessing the degree of relatedness – a **kin-recognition** module. This must have played a vital part in the system of modules governing the provision of favours and help to others.

SUPPOSE THE CHANCES OF BEING REPAID WERE LOW OR NIL?

THEN THE SOCIAL-COOPERATION MODULE MIGHT CONSULT THE KIN-RECOGNITION MODULE TO SEE WHETHER THE POTENTIAL BENEFICIARY WAS A RELATIVE OR NOT.

IF THEY WERE, THEN HELP COULD BE PROVIDED WITHOUT ANY EXPECTATION THAT IT WOULD BE RETURNED.

Alliances and cooperation would therefore have been more likely to develop between close relatives than between unrelated individuals. In other words, evolutionary psychology predicts that humans should have instinctual tendencies towards nepotism.

The Truth About Cinderella

In the 1980s, two Canadian psychologists, **Martin Daly** and **Margo Wilson**, set out to test this Darwinian prediction. In one study, they compared the childcare provided by natural parents and by step-parents. Step-parents are in a very unusual situation from an evolutionary point of view. They are caring for a child who they know is not their own. Even though they may care for the child conscientiously, evolutionary theory predicts that the childcare modules will not be activated in the same way as in biological parents. But is this true?

Looking for a way to compare the parental love shown by biological parents and step-parents, Daly and Wilson reasoned that, since love inhibits violence, those with greater love would show, on average, lower levels of violence.

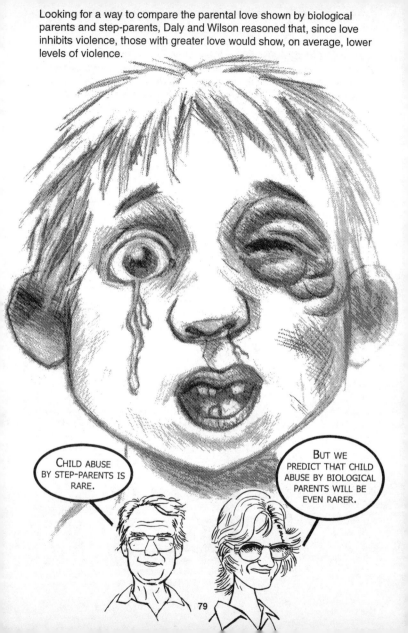

CHILD ABUSE BY STEP-PARENTS IS RARE.

BUT WE PREDICT THAT CHILD ABUSE BY BIOLOGICAL PARENTS WILL BE EVEN RARER.

When Daly and Wilson looked at statistics of child abuse in North America, they found a striking confirmation of the Darwinian prediction. In the USA, they found that a child living with one or more substitute parents was about 100 times as likely to be fatally abused as a child living with natural parents only. A similar pattern was observed in Canada, where statistics showed that, for children of two or younger, the risk of being killed by a step-parent was about 70 times that from a natural parent. These data provide strong support for the existence of childcare modules in humans that help parents to recognize their own children and to channel parental investment preferentially towards them.

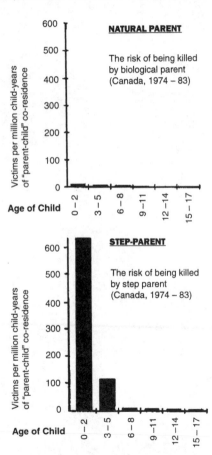

Allocating Resources to Offspring

Another problem that parents face, besides that of distinguishing their own children from those of others, is the problem of resource allocation. Parents have limited time, energy and food, and they must decide how much of these precious resources to give to each of their children, and how much to use for their own survival.

PARENTS WHO ALLOCATE MINIMAL RESOURCES TO THEIR CHILDREN WILL SURVIVE FOR LONGER THAN MORE GENEROUS PARENTS.

BUT THE CHILDREN OF THE STINGY PARENTS WILL HAVE LESS CHANCE OF SURVIVING, AND SO LESS CHANCE OF PASSING ON THE PARENTS' GENES.

SO IT PAYS PARENTS TO BE GENEROUS TO THEIR CHILDREN.

On the other hand, parents who are so generous that they compromise their own survival risk dying and having no more offspring. There is a trade-off, then, between parental generosity, which raises the survival chances of *actual* offspring, and parental withholding, which raises the survival chances of *future* offspring.

The Resource-Allocation Module

We should expect natural selection to have designed special mental machinery for calculating the optimal amount of resources to allocate to each child at any given moment. This resource-allocation module will have to take into account a number of decisive factors.

Parent-Offspring Conflict

The problem of allocating resources to children is made more complicated by the fact that the children themselves may disagree with their parents about how much they should be given. Children may want more than their parents are prepared to give. The evolutionary basis for this was set out by the American biologist **Robert Trivers** in 1974, in a famous paper on "Parent-Offspring Conflict".

Trivers argued that the crux of the matter lies with the fact that a child is *twice* as related to itself as it is to its siblings. Everyone is 100% genetically related to himself, but only 50% related to his brothers and sisters.

So, even though you care about your brothers and sisters, you care about yourself even more. From the parents' point of view, though, things are somewhat different. Parents have the same degree of relatedness to all their children, and so value them all equally. This is the source of parent-offspring conflict.

How Much For Me?

To illustrate the problem, imagine a mother who wants to divide a cake between her two children. The children are equally related to her, so, other things being equal, she should cut the cake in half. But now think of it from the point of view of each child. Each child has a genetic stake in the welfare of the other child.

Each child is 100% related to itself, but only 50% related to its sibling, so (other things being equal) each child should want twice as much cake for itself as for its sibling. If the child could divide the cake up, it should give a third to the sibling, and keep two thirds for itself.

Weaning

This simplified example illustrates the general principle behind the evolutionary theory of parent-offspring conflict. The conflicts arise because children always want slightly more than what their parents think is their "fair share". Take weaning, for example. No child wants to breast-feed forever.

There comes a time when the benefit that a child derives from the mother's milk is less than half the benefit that a younger sibling would gain from the same milk.

The Benefit of Weaning

So a point does come when it is in the child's genetic interest to seek alternative sources of nourishment, and let a younger sibling have the mother's milk to itself. The problem is that this point in time is always later than the point at which the mother comes to the same conclusion. The mother wants to wean the child when the benefit it gains from breastfeeding is *less than the benefit* that a younger sibling would gain.

So the mother always wants to wean the child before the child wants to wean itself.

Mind-reading Modules

We have seen that the various modules for social exchange evolved to help our primate ancestors solve the free-rider problem. This enabled them to form the stable alliances that hold together the social groups in which all higher primates live. But the increasing size of these groups posed a problem in itself – a problem which was solved by learning how to "mind-read".

I WONDER WHAT SHE'S THINKING ...

Of course, we don't read other people's minds by direct telepathy. This is not what evolutionary psychologists mean by "mind-reading". Mind-reading involves guessing what people are thinking on the basis of observing their actions and their words.

Group Size and Social Intelligence

The size of the groups in which our ancestors lived increased dramatically during the course of hominid evolution. Around six million years ago, when our ancestors resembled modern chimpanzees, the average group size was about 50. By three million years ago, our "australopithecine" ancestors were living in groups of about 70. A million years later, our "habiline" (tool-making) ancestors were living in groups of about 80. The first true humans (*Homo sapiens sapiens*), who emerged around 150,000 years ago, probably lived in groups of around 150.

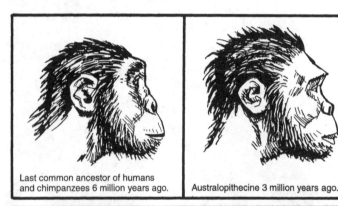

Last common ancestor of humans and chimpanzees 6 million years ago.

Australopithecine 3 million years ago.

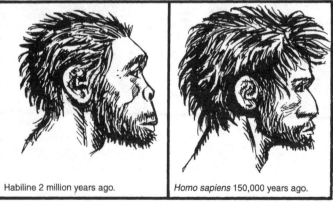

Habiline 2 million years ago.

Homo sapiens 150,000 years ago.

As groups got bigger, the problems posed by group living got more complex. Not only did our ancestors need bigger memories to keep track of the fast-changing pattern of alliances in the group, but they also needed more sophisticated social reasoning capacities to maintain a delicate balance between their conflicting loyalties.

Enter Machiavelli

This idea is known as the "Machiavellian intelligence" hypothesis, after **Niccolò Machiavelli** (1469-1527), the infamous Italian political theorist. Machiavelli's book *The Prince* (1514) outlines some of the dirty tricks that successful politicians use to obtain and maintain power. The Machiavellian intelligence hypothesis starts from the idea that these dirty tricks are not just the preserve of politicians.

WE ALL USE THEM IN OUR EVERYDAY LIFE, AS WE HELP OUR FRIENDS AND ATTEMPT TO OUTSMART OUR ENEMIES, MAKE (AND BREAK) PROMISES, AND TELL LIES.

I WROTE ABOUT MACHIAVELLIAN INTELLIGENCE IN 1975.

NICK HUMPHREY

THE PRINCE NICCOLO MACHIAVELLI

Even this "everyday politics" requires a fairly sophisticated understanding of human psychology – in particular, a special mental module for "reading other people's minds".

Theory of Mind

This "mind-reading module" is usually referred to by evolutionary psychologists as the "Theory of Mind" module. This is because it seems to operate on the basis of a theory of how the human mind works. The theory that the module uses is, apparently, the very same theory that we find in "folk psychology" and in cognitive science – the "belief/desire" theory which states that actions are caused by mental processes like beliefs and desires.

Folk Psychology

In other words, folk psychology is not just a cultural invention. It is an innate part of the human mind. Adults do not *teach* children to understand human behaviour in terms of beliefs and desires. Rather, children instinctively *develop* the ability to do this, because they are genetically programmed to do so.

I CAN ALREADY READ OTHER PEOPLE'S MINDS!

The Theory of Mind module develops during the first years of life, and is usually complete by the age of four-and-a-half. At that age, children can pass "false-belief tests".

A classic false-belief test is the so-called "Sally-Ann" test. A psychologist introduces a child to two dolls called Sally and Ann. Then the child watches while Sally puts some sweets under a cushion and leaves the room. While Sally is out of the room, Ann takes the sweets from under the cushion and puts them in her pocket. When Sally comes back into the room, the psychologist questions the child.

WHERE DOES SALLY THINK THE SWEETS ARE?

IN ANN'S POCKET!

Before the age of four-and-a-half, this is what children usually say. Lacking a fully-developed Theory of Mind, they cannot comprehend the notion that other people can hold beliefs that are different from their own. They assume that everyone believes what they believe.

Theory of Mind and Autism

After the age of four-and-a-half, children respond very differently to the Sally-Ann test. When asked where Sally thinks the sweets are, they now reply, "Under the cushion".

I KNOW THE SWEETS ARE IN ANN'S POCKETS, BUT I NOW HAVE A FULLY-DEVELOPED THEORY OF MIND.

SO THEY UNDERSTAND THAT OTHER PEOPLE CAN HOLD BELIEFS THAT DIFFER FROM THEIR OWN. THEY ALSO UNDERSTAND THAT THESE BELIEFS CAN BE FALSE.

AUTISM OCCURS WHEN CHILDREN FAIL TO DEVELOP A PROPERLY FUNCTIONING THEORY OF MIND MODULE.

According to the British psychologist **Simon Baron-Cohen**, autistic people are "mindblind".

Lying and Tactical Deception

Without a Theory of Mind, it would be very difficult to play the political games necessary for living in human society. For one thing, it would be impossible to lie.

IN ORDER TO LIE, YOU MUST FIRST UNDERSTAND THAT OTHER PEOPLE CAN HOLD DIFFERENT BELIEFS FROM YOURS.

AND THOSE BELIEFS CAN BE FALSE.

Only then can you attempt to manipulate another person into holding a false belief. This is why children under the age of three cannot lie convincingly.

Language Modules

All animals that regularly interact with other members of their own species face the problem of communicating with each other. Different species solve this problem in different ways, but many use sounds because, unlike visual signals, sounds can be perceived at night and over long distances. All primates use their vocal cords to produce different kinds of signals to convey different kinds of information. Humans, however, have evolved the most sophisticated communication system in the animal kingdom – language.

The Language Acquisition Device

Special mental machinery is required in order to learn and use a human language. We have already seen how Chomsky's work in the 1950s and 60s showed that it would be impossible for children to learn a language as quickly as they do unless they were pre-programmed to do so. In other words, all children must be born with a special-purpose language-learning program, or Language Acquisition Device.

The Language Acquisition Device is unique to humans.

SOME PRIMATOLOGISTS ARGUE THAT CHIMPANZEES ALSO HAVE THE CAPACITY TO ACQUIRE LANGUAGE.

BUT MOST LINGUISTS REJECT THIS VIEW.

IS THAT ALL HE CAN SAY – ASK FOR A BANANA?

Despite valiant attempts to teach them to use English and sign language, chimpanzees have never succeeded in learning more than a few dozen words and producing a few very simple sentences. Human children, on the other hand, learn thousands of words and master the most complex rules of grammar by the age of five.

The Evolution of Language

No one knows when our ancestors acquired the capacity to use language, but it must have been before they moved out of Africa, some 100,000 years ago. After that time, different human groups became separated from each other for thousands of years. If the language modules evolved after the emigration from Africa, it would mean that exactly the same mental machinery had evolved independently in all the different human groups. This is extremely unlikely.

Anatomical studies suggest that the capacity to use language evolved between 300,000 and 200,000 years ago. It was then that the position of the larynx changed to its current position, which is much lower down than the larynx of other primates. The lower larynx of humans enables them to produce a much wider range of sounds. The lower tracheal opening is also responsible for the human capacity for choking. Our ability to speak was only purchased at the price of an increased risk of asphyxiating on our food.

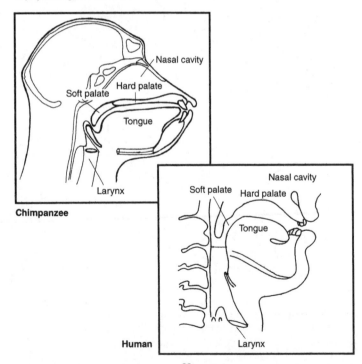

Chimpanzee

Human

Why did our ancestors evolve such a sophisticated communication system? One theory is that it enabled them to hunt more effectively. According to this view, the primary function of language was to exchange information about the physical and ecological environment. In 1993, the British anthropologist, **Robin Dunbar**, challenged this theory. Dunbar suggested that the primary function of language was to exchange information about the *social* environment.

Reciprocal Altruism Again

Dunbar's argument was based on the observation that, some time between 500,000 and 200,000 years ago, our ancestors began to live in much larger groups than before. Dunbar estimated that group size increased to about 150 individuals. We have already seen how primate groups are held together by networks of alliances formed by reciprocal altruism.

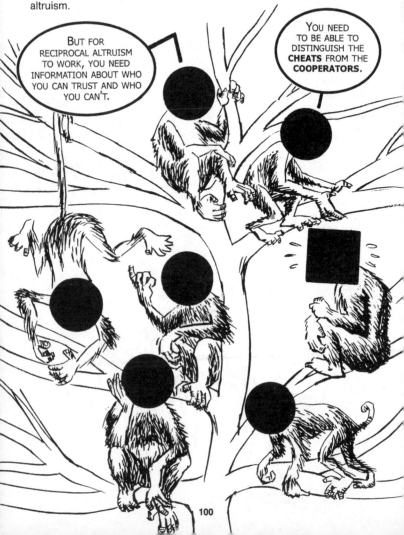

Chimps gain this information by direct personal interaction, especially grooming. They spend large amounts of time removing fleas and dirt from each other's backs, and this mutual grooming is the social cement that holds their alliances together. A chimp in trouble is far more likely to receive help from a grooming partner than any other chimp.

Since reciprocal altruism depends on having direct interactions with others, there are limits to the size of the group that can be held together by this mechanism. There is a limit to the number of people you can meet and interact with on a regular enough basis to get information about how likely they are to cooperate.

Gossip

Dunbar argued that language evolved to provide our ancestors with another way to get the valuable social information about who you can trust. Instead of discovering whether someone is a cheat the hard way – by being cheated – our ancestors were able to find this out by talking to other people. In Dunbar's view, the first function of language was gossip. This might explain why humans are so fascinated by gossip about other people's behaviour.

FLINTSTONE WENT NUTS WHEN HE HEARD HIS WIFE WAS CHEATING ON HIM ...

YOU DON'T SAY ...

Indirect Reciprocity

By facilitating the exchange of social information, language enabled humans to reap the rewards of living in larger groups. Reciprocal altruism could hold these larger groups together because it no longer needed to be direct.

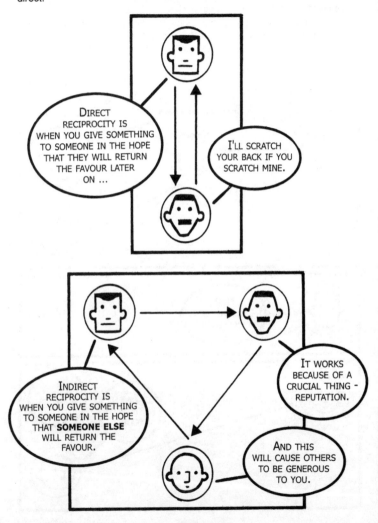

The Importance of Reputation

If other people see or hear about your acts of generosity, and if other people tend to be generous to those with a good reputation, then it pays you to be generous. Even if the recipient of a favour never returns the favour directly, it will get you a good reputation. And this will cause others to be generous to you. On the other hand, if you are not generous, you will acquire a reputation for stinginess. And others will punish you for this by being stingy to you. I won't scratch your back if you don't scratch theirs.

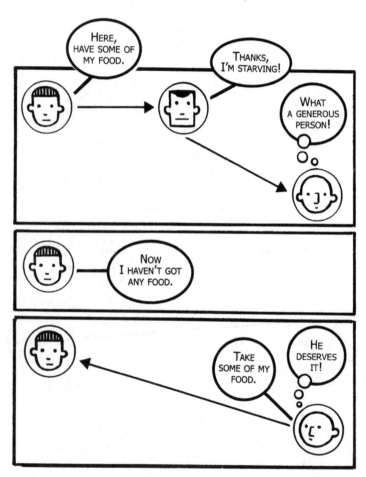

Mate-Selection Modules

Most of the adaptive problems that we have discussed so far – avoiding predators, eating the right food, forming alliances, reading other people's minds and communicating with other people – relate to the fundamental problem of survival. But while an organism's survival is vitally important from the genes' point of view, there is something even more important.

From the gene's point of view, the survival of the organism is merely a means to this end. If an organism lives for a hundred years, but has no offspring, this is of no use to the genes.

The Mating Game

Some species reproduce by dividing into two parts, each of which becomes a separate individual. In these "asexual" species, there is no need to find a mate, since you can reproduce without one. Most species, however, reproduce sexually. This involves finding a mate and swapping genes with them. Biologists still disagree about why sex evolved. Most argue that sexual reproduction confers some advantage to the individual organism, but there is no consensus about what this advantage is.

Humans are a sexually-reproducing species. In order for us to reproduce, we must first find a mate.

FINDING A MATE IS NOT AN EASY TASK.

FIRST, YOU MUST CHOOSE A SUITABLE CANDIDATE FROM AMONG THE MANY POSSIBLE MATES AVAILABLE.

SECOND, YOU MUST PERSUADE AT LEAST ONE OF THEM TO CHOOSE YOU.

We should expect natural selection to have designed special mental mechanisms that enabled our ancestors to solve the problems specific to choosing and obtaining a suitable mate. Selecting a suitable mate is very important because mates provide two things on which the survival of your offspring depends: genes and parental care. The survival chances of offspring depend on the quality of these two resources. We will now look at each of them in more detail.

The Genes are in the Selection

The first way in which your mate affects the survival chances of your offspring is by providing – or failing to provide – good genes. In a sexually-reproducing species, offspring inherit 50% of their genes from each parent. If you mate with someone who has bad genes ("bad" in the sense that they lower your chances of surviving and reproducing), your offspring will probably inherit some of these bad genes. That will lower their chances of surviving and reproducing.

WE MAY NOT LIVE TO PASS ON THE GENES THAT WE INHERITED FROM YOU.

BUT IF I MATE WITH SOMEONE WHO HAS GOOD GENES ...

WE WILL PROBABLY INHERIT SOME OF THESE GOOD GENES.

That will raise their chances of surviving and reproducing, and so raise the chances of your genes getting passed on to future generations.

The Importance of Looking Good

How did our ancestors solve the problem of selecting mates with good genes and avoiding those with bad genes?

Physical appearances provide important clues to the quality of one's genes.

Body Symmetry

For example, the more symmetrical your body is, the better on average your genes are. This is because less robust genes are more likely to get knocked off course by environmental setbacks such as physical injuries and parasites.

Anyone who was sensitive to small differences in bodily symmetry, and who preferred to mate with more symmetrical people, would tend to have children with better genes. So we would expect natural selection to have designed a mate-selection module that was geared to detect and prefer more symmetrical mates.

What's the Evidence for Symmetry?

Is there any evidence to show that humans do, in fact, prefer more symmetrical mates? There is. The psychologist **Steve Gangestad** and the biologist **Randy Thornhill** measured various features, from foot breadth and hand breadth to ear length and ear breadth, and combined these measurements to produce an overall index of bodily symmetry for each person in their study.

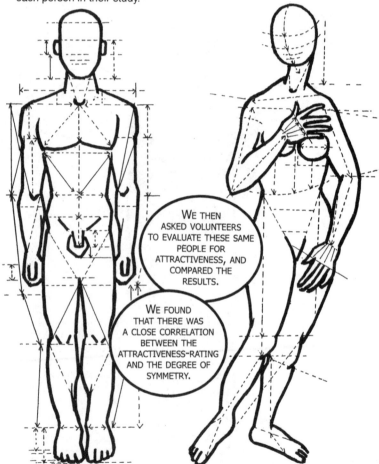

WE THEN ASKED VOLUNTEERS TO EVALUATE THESE SAME PEOPLE FOR ATTRACTIVENESS, AND COMPARED THE RESULTS.

WE FOUND THAT THERE WAS A CLOSE CORRELATION BETWEEN THE ATTRACTIVENESS-RATING AND THE DEGREE OF SYMMETRY.

More symmetrical people were seen as more attractive.

The Biology of Beauty

Many people today think that standards of beauty are entirely cultural artefacts. But in the past few decades, evidence has increasingly emerged to show that there are many aesthetic preferences that are both universal and innate. Preferences for more symmetrical people, for example, are universal.

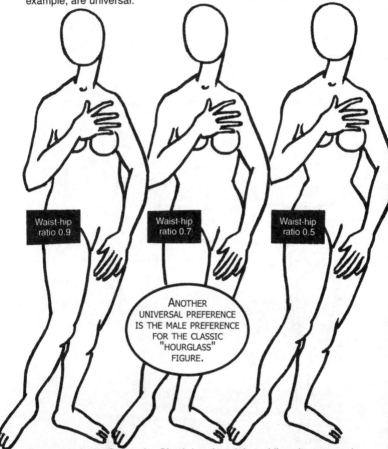

Waist-hip ratio 0.9

Waist-hip ratio 0.7

Waist-hip ratio 0.5

ANOTHER UNIVERSAL PREFERENCE IS THE MALE PREFERENCE FOR THE CLASSIC "HOURGLASS" FIGURE.

The psychologist **Devendra Singh** has found that while cultures vary in their view of the ideal weight for women, the ideal waist-hip ratio is always the same – people everywhere rate a waist-hip ratio of 0.7 as the most attractive. This is the classic "hourglass figure".

The Fertility Factor

Why has natural selection endowed men with a preference for the hourglass figure? Because the waist-hip ratio is a good indicator of **fertility**. Women with a 0.7 waist-hip ratio tend to be more fertile than those who have a higher or lower waist-hip ratio. This is a clear example of the way that natural selection has sculpted men's sense of beauty.

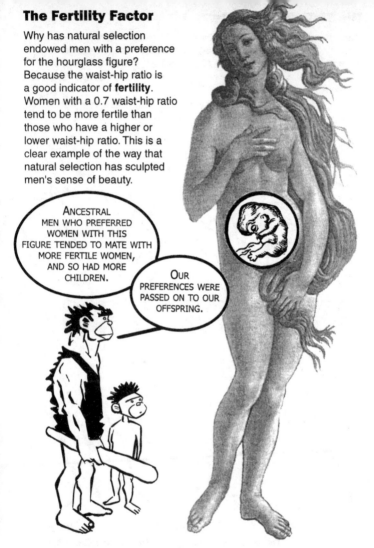

ANCESTRAL MEN WHO PREFERRED WOMEN WITH THIS FIGURE TENDED TO MATE WITH MORE FERTILE WOMEN, AND SO HAD MORE CHILDREN.

OUR PREFERENCES WERE PASSED ON TO OUR OFFSPRING.

Just as natural selection endowed us with appetites to make us seek out the most nutritious foods, so it endowed us with a sense of beauty to make us seek out mates with high-quality genes.

Selecting a Mate for Parental Care

The other way in which your mate affects the survival chances of
your offspring is by providing – or failing to provide – parental care.
Not all sexually-reproducing species care for their young. In some
species, the offspring are left to fend for themselves as soon as they
are born. Of the species that do care for their young, most leave
the task entirely to the mother.

WHEN MY BABY IS BORN, I LOOK AFTER IT ON MY OWN, WITHOUT ANY HELP FROM THE FATHER.

WITH HUMANS, IT IS MUCH MORE COMMON FOR FATHERS TO TAKE AN ACTIVE ROLE IN PROVIDING PROTECTION AND RESOURCES FOR THEIR CHILDREN.

In the jargon of evolutionary biology, the human species shows an
unusually high level of "male parental investment".

Human Pair Bonds

Human children, then, are typically cared for not just by a single mother, but by a mother and father together.

Parental Care and Human Brain Size

This probably played an important part in the massive increase in brain size that took place during the past few million years of human evolution. Big brains are expensive organs that take time to develop.

Graph Showing the Increase in Brain Volume During the Past Four Million Years of Human Evolution

Second "spurt" of brain enlargement, 500,000 – 200,000 years ago.

First "spurt" of brain enlargement, 2.0 – 1.5 million years ago.

Brain Volume (mm³)

The Present Day

Millions of Years Ago

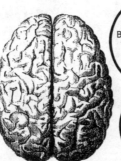

DURING THIS TIME, THE INFANT CANNOT TAKE CARE OF ITSELF AND MUST BE LOOKED AFTER BY OTHERS.

HUMANS HAVE BIGGER BRAINS, RELATIVE TO THE SIZE OF THEIR BODIES, THAN ANY OTHER ANIMAL.

HUMAN INFANTS THUS TAKE LONGER TO BECOME INDEPENDENT THAN THE OFFSPRING OF ANY OTHER SPECIES.

The time and energy required to care for a growing human infant cannot be provided by a single parent acting alone.

Will You Make a Good Parent?

When choosing a mate, therefore, our ancestors had to consider not just the quality of the mate's genes, but also the mate's capacity and willingness to invest time and energy in helping to bring up the children.

If you want to get information about whether someone will make a good parent or not, you have to pay attention to their *behaviour*, not their physical appearance.

parent? Parenting is a cooperative venture, a particular kind of
alliance, so the same criteria that allow us to decide who will be
a good ally in general can be used to determine if someone will
make a good parent for one's own children.

> ANYTHING THAT INDICATES KINDNESS, PATIENCE, GENEROSITY AND TRUSTWORTHINESS WILL BE A USEFUL CLUE TO PARENTING ABILITY.

> SO NATURAL SELECTION SHOULD HAVE FAVOURED THE INCORPORATION OF THESE CRITERIA IN THE MATE-SELECTION MODULE.

And there is evidence that this is indeed the case. All over the world,
people of both sexes say that these are the characteristics they most

Sex Differences in Mate Preferences

The minds of men and women are largely identical, because most of the adaptive problems faced by our ancestors were the same for men and women. The problem of avoiding predators was largely the same for both sexes, as was the problem of eating the right food, the problem of forming alliances, and the problem of mind-reading.

SO WE SHOULD EXPECT THE MODULES CONCERNED WITH THESE TASKS TO BE LARGELY IDENTICAL IN BOTH SEXES.

FINE. BUT WHEN IT COMES TO CHOOSING A PARTNER – WHAT THEN?

What about the mate-selection modules? Do men and women differ in their mate preferences? Many of the problems involved in choosing a long-term mate were identical for both sexes.

These different problems required different solutions, and so we should expect the mate-selection modules of men and women to reflect these differences.

Dads and Cads

Choosing a mate poses different problems for men and women because the same reproductive strategies are not available to both sexes. Both sexes can look for a long-term partner and establish a pair-bond with them to rear children together. Biologists refer to this as a "long-term mating strategy", and it is the same for both men and women. The alternative is the "short-term mating strategy". This option is also available to both sexes, but not in the same way.

FOR US, THE SHORT-TERM MATING STRATEGY INVOLVES HAVING SEX WITH A WOMAN AND THEN ABANDONING HER TO LOOK AFTER THE BABY.

CLEARLY, THIS IS NOT A VIABLE OPTION FOR **US**, BECAUSE IT IS WOMEN, NOT MEN, WHO GET PREGNANT.

This difference between men and women posed an adaptive problem for ancestral women. They had to be able to tell the difference between a man who was pursuing a long-term mating strategy and a man who was pursuing a short-term mating strategy. Women who could not tell the difference ran the risk of becoming single mothers, which lowered their child's chances of survival. Natural selection endowed women with various mental mechanisms to help them avoid this fate. One such mechanism lies behind the delaying tactics of women. Women tend to be more cautious than men about having sex.

In ancestral environments, this was a way of making sure that the man was interested in a long-term relationship and was not simply looking for a one-night stand.

Battle of the Sexes – or Evolutionary Arms Race?

However, if ancestral women had never agreed to have sex without looking for signs of commitment from the man, then natural selection would have eliminated those men who could not show signs of commitment.

WE WOULD NEVER HAVE BEEN ABLE TO HAVE SEX – SO OUR GENES WOULD HAVE QUICKLY DIED OUT.

PERHAPS SOME OF US WOULD HAVE BECOME GOOD AT TRICKING WOMEN INTO HAVING SEX BY FEIGNING COMMITMENT AND THEN DESERTING.

BUT THEN NATURAL SELECTION WOULD HAVE FAVOURED THOSE OF US WHO WERE GOOD AT DETECTING LIARS – AND THE LIARS WOULD HAVE BEEN ELIMINATED.

The Myth of the Monogamous Female

Since the male tendency to pursue casual sex has clearly not died out, this must be because ancestral women were not completely monogamous either. The idea that men only want casual sex, while women only want commitment, is not supported by evolutionary psychology.

Women's Extra-Pair Mating

But what advantages could *women* derive from casual sex? If women did not have the option of leaving men holding the baby, why would they have bothered with a short-term mating strategy?

ONE POSSIBILITY IS THAT ANCESTRAL WOMEN MAY HAVE USED THE SHORT-TERM MATING STRATEGY FOR PURPOSES OTHER THAN REPRODUCTION.

FOR EXAMPLE, ANCESTRAL WOMEN MAY HAVE SWAPPED SEX FOR FOOD, MUCH AS CHIMPANZEES DO TODAY.

…ther possibility is that an ancestral woman who was already in a …g-term relationship might have had casual sex with other men and …n passed the resulting children off as her partner's.

…is is the female version of the short-term mating strategy

What's the Best Strategy?

Even with these potential benefits, however, casual sex was still riskier for ancestral women than for ancestral men. Those women without a long-term partner could still be left holding the baby, and those with a long-term partner ran the risk of being discovered and punished. So natural selection favoured women who were more cautious about having casual sex than men.

EVEN THOUGH BOTH SEXES USE BOTH LONG-TERM AND SHORT-TERM MATING STRATEGIES ...

... THEY DO NOT USE THEM TO THE SAME EXTENT.

Men are more inclined to pursue the short-term strategy than women because it is less costly and the benefits are potentially much greater to them. A man who has sex with a thousand women can potentially have a thousand children. But a woman can only have a few children in her lifetime, no matter how many men she has sex with.

Men with Resources

Because women preferred a long-term mating strategy, men who did not look as if they would be good fathers were less successful in the mating game. So natural selection favoured men who looked as if they would be good fathers. What are the things that make a man a good father? In the world of the stone-age, a key factor in being a good father was being able to provide resources for the child. So females should have evolved preferences for men with the capacity to acquire costly resources. Mae West, the diva of film comedy, summed it up.

Testing Mate Preferences

In the 1980s, an American psychologist called **David Buss** set out to test these evolutionary predictions about mate preferences. If mate preferences have evolved by natural selection, they should be cross-cultural and universal. So Buss and his team carried out interviews with over 10,000 people in 33 countries located on six continents and five islands.

In one experiment, women stated that they were unwilling to go out with, have sex, or marry the men in low-status costumes, but were willing to consider all these relationships with men in high-status clothes, even though it was the same man in all the pictures.

WE FOUND THAT IN **EVERY** COUNTRY, WOMEN VALUED "GOOD FINANCIAL PROSPECTS" IN A POTENTIAL MATE MORE HIGHLY THAN MEN DID.

THE EVOLUTIONARY PREDICTION ABOUT FEMALE PREFERENCE FOR MEN WITH RESOURCES WAS CONFIRMED.

As with most studies of differences between men and women, the data obtained by Buss showed a big overlap in the scores of each sex. Nevertheless, the difference between the average of all male values and the average of all female values was often statistically significant. When discussing the differences between men and women, it is important to remember that we are talking about averages of groups, and not individuals. Some men are shorter than some women, but it is still true that men are, on average, taller than women, and that difference needs explaining.

Attractiveness and Age

Buss's survey also showed that, all over the world, women prefer mates older than they are. This may also be related to the female preference for men with the capacity to acquire resources.

MEN TEND TO GET BETTER AT ACQUIRING RESOURCES AS THEY GET OLDER.

MEN, ON THE OTHER HAND, UNIVERSALLY PREFER YOUNGER MATES.

The evolutionary explanation for this is that reproductive success is much more related to age in women than it is in men.

Age and Reproduction

Sperm counts do decline slightly as a man gets older, but a man can still have children when he is eighty. In women, on the other hand, fertility reaches a peak in the early twenties, declines rapidly after the age of thirty, and ceases absolutely at menopause (which probably occurred in the forties during the stone-age, when our diets were less nutritious). So it is much more important for a man to find a young mate.

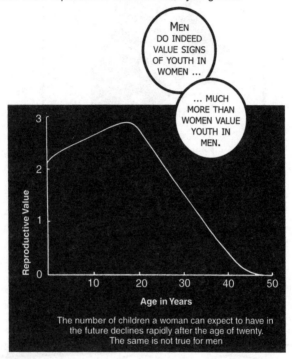

The number of children a woman can expect to have in the future declines rapidly after the age of twenty. The same is not true for men

Men prefer mates who have physical features associated with youth – such as smooth skin, good muscle tone, lustrous hair, and full lips – as well as behavioural clues, such as high energy level.

WHEN LOOKING FOR A LONG-TERM PARTNER, RATHER THAN FOR CASUAL SEX, BOTH MEN AND WOMEN LOOK FOR SOMEONE WHO CAN BE FAITHFUL.

HOWEVER, MEN PLACE A HIGHER VALUE ON SEXUAL FIDELITY THAN WOMEN DO BECAUSE THE RISKS ARE GREATER.

If a man has sex with another woman, this poses a threat to his partner because the man might divert some of his resources to the other woman. But if a woman has sex with another man, this poses an even greater threat to *her* partner because the woman might get pregnant, and her partner might end up investing lots of time and energy in caring for another man's child.

131

Male and Female Jealousy

Because female infidelity is a greater threat to male reproductive success than male infidelity is to female reproductive success, men should have evolved to be more concerned about sexual fidelity than women. This does seem to be the case.

EXPERIMENTS HAVE SHOWN THAT WHEN WOMEN GET JEALOUS, THEY ARE MORE CONCERNED ABOUT THEIR PARTNER'S AFFECTIONS FOR OTHER WOMEN.

MEN TEND TO BE MORE CONCERNED ABOUT THEIR PARTNERS HAVING SEX WITH SOMEONE ELSE.

This pattern fits the evolutionary theory exactly, which predicts that women should be more concerned about their partner diverting resources away to another person, while men should be more concerned about the possibility of being duped into caring for a child that is not their own.

Mapping the Mind

This concludes our survey of some of the modules in the human mind. We have only scratched the surface, however. According to Cosmides and Tooby, there are hundreds, perhaps thousands, of modules.

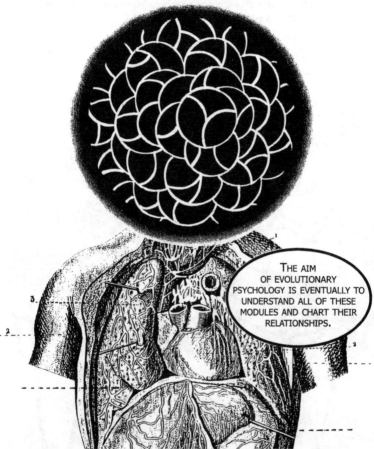

THE AIM OF EVOLUTIONARY PSYCHOLOGY IS EVENTUALLY TO UNDERSTAND ALL OF THESE MODULES AND CHART THEIR RELATIONSHIPS.

When this has been achieved, we will be able to produce a complete map of the human mind. Just as anatomy textbooks contain diagrams of the human body, complete with all the organs and physiological systems, so psychology textbooks will one day contain diagrams of the human mind, complete with all the modules.

Criticisms of Evolutionary Psychology

Despite the fact that evolutionary psychology is based on two of the most successful scientific theories ever developed – evolutionary biology and cognitive psychology – it has many critics. In the last part of this book, we shall look at some of these criticisms and show how evolutionary psychologists have responded to them.

The critics accuse evolutionary psychology of the following three things.

PAN-ADAPTATIONISM
Stephen Jay Gould

REDUCTIONISM
Richard Lewontin

GENETIC DETERMINISM
Steven Rose

Pan-adaptationism

As we have already seen, the concept of adaptation is central to evolutionary biology and evolutionary psychology.

Side-effects and By-products

Not all biological traits are adaptations, however – some are just side-effects or by-products of traits that *are* adaptations. For example, the complex structure of bones is an adaptation that solves the problem of providing a strong but light framework on which soft tissue can be arranged.

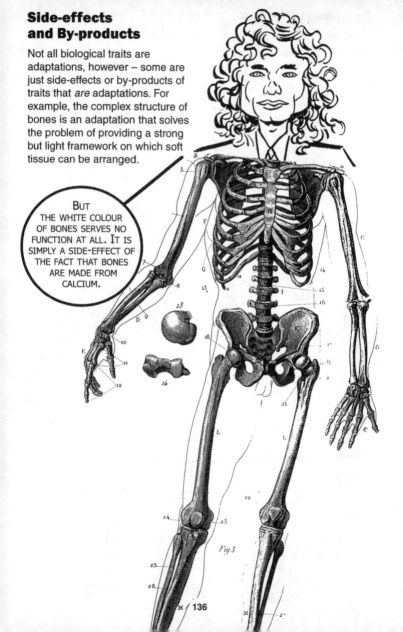

BUT THE WHITE COLOUR OF BONES SERVES NO FUNCTION AT ALL. IT IS SIMPLY A SIDE-EFFECT OF THE FACT THAT BONES ARE MADE FROM CALCIUM.

Not Everything is a Module

The same point applies to the mind. Mental modules are adaptations, but there are many other mental phenomena that are just by-products of these adaptations. Take reading, for example. The capacity to read was not directly designed by natural selection. Writing was only invented some 5,000 years ago, which is not nearly enough time for natural selection to design a complex adaptation.

THERE IS NO "READING MODULE" IN THE HUMAN MIND.

The first writing? These two stone tablets were found in Syria.

The capacity to read must therefore be a side-effect of various other modules that were designed by natural selection – such as the modules for vision and language.

Hypotheses and Confirmations

This means that evolutionary psychologists must be careful when attempting to map the mind. They must not assume that there is a module for every complex capacity, because some capacities are just side-effects of modules designed for other things.

IF THEY THINK THAT SOME BEHAVIOUR IS CAUSED BY A MODULE DESIGNED TO PRODUCE THAT BEHAVIOUR, THEY MUST DEVISE A WAY OF TESTING THEIR IDEA.

UNTIL THEY TEST IT, THE IDEA REMAINS JUST A HYPOTHESIS.

There is nothing wrong with hypotheses, of course. The way scientists discover new things is by inventing new hypotheses and then testing them. If the tests confirm the hypothesis, it becomes part of our scientific knowledge. If the tests refute the hypothesis, it is rejected and the scientists try to come up with alternative hypotheses. This is just good scientific practice.

WHAT IS **NOT** GOOD SCIENTIFIC PRACTICE IS TO ACCEPT A HYPOTHESIS BEFORE IT HAS BEEN PROPERLY TESTED.

Just-So Stories?

Some critics accuse evolutionary psychologists of this scientific sin. The American palaeontologist **Stephen Jay Gould**, for example, has claimed that evolutionary psychologists are too ready to believe in evolutionary explanations for human behaviours.

> EVOLUTIONARY PSYCHOLOGISTS ACCEPT ADAPTIVE HYPOTHESES JUST BECAUSE THEY ARE GOOD STORIES, WITHOUT PROPERLY TESTING THEM.

Gould thinks that this leads evolutionary psychologists to forget that many mental phenomena are just side-effects (which Gould calls "spandrels"). The name for this tendency to believe that **everything** is an adaptation is "pan-adaptationism".

Are evolutionary psychologists guilty of pan-adaptationism? Do they really forget that many mental phenomena are just side-effects? All the evidence points the opposite way. Evolutionary psychologists are reluctant to call something an adaptation unless there is firm evidence to show that it is. In this, evolutionary psychologists follow the rule of thumb put forward by the American biologist **George Williams** in his 1966 book, *Adaptation and Natural Selection*.

ADAPTATION IS A SPECIAL AND ONEROUS CONCEPT THAT SHOULD BE USED ONLY WHERE IT IS REALLY NECESSARY.

ADAPTATION AND NATURAL SELECTION
George Williams
1966

Evolutionary psychologists accept that much of human behaviour today is a side-effect of modules designed for other things. Humans today play computer games, build aeroplanes, and do hundreds of other things that our ancestors did not do.

THE ABILITIES TO DO THESE THINGS ARE NOT TO BE EXPLAINED BY POSTULATING MODULES FOR COMPUTER GAMES AND BUILDING AEROPLANES.

THESE ABILITIES ARE BY-PRODUCTS OF MODULES WITH OTHER FUNCTIONS.

In fact, most of the great products of human civilization – including art, religion and science – are probably side-effects of modules that were originally designed for other purposes. Perhaps the greatest challenge for evolutionary psychology is to show exactly *how* a mind that was designed for life in the stone-age is capable of such extraordinary cultural achievements.

Is Logic a By-product?

A good example of an evolutionary analysis of a cognitive side-effect is provided by Leda Cosmides and John Tooby.

MANY OF OUR MENTAL CAPACITIES FOR ABSTRACT REASONING THAT PERMIT MODERN HUMANS TO SOLVE COMPLEX LOGICAL PROBLEMS ...

... ARE BY-PRODUCTS OF THE MODULES INVOLVED IN REGULATING SOCIAL **EXCHANGE.**

WHAT DOES LOGIC HAVE TO DO WITH "SOCIAL EXCHANGE"? WHAT'S YOUR EVIDENCE?

Some evidence to support Cosmides and Tooby's claim comes from the results of a psychological test called the Wason-selection task. See if you can do it on the next page.

The Wason-selection Task

There is a pack of cards which have numbers on one side and letters on the other. Four of these cards are placed on the table in front of you as follows:

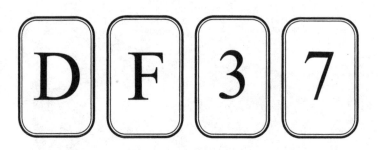

You are told that the following rule applies: *If a card has a "D" on one side, then it has a "3" on the other side.*

WHICH CARDS DO YOU NEED TO TURN OVER TO FIND OUT IF THIS IS TRUE?

Most people give the wrong answer when presented with the problem in this way. But when Cosmides and Tooby changed the way the task was presented, most people got the right answer. Their version of the task is on the next page …

You are the bouncer in a bar. You must make sure that no under-age drinkers drink beer. Each card is a customer; it says the customer's age on one side, and what he or she is drinking on the other side. Now which cards do you have to turn over?

DRINKING BEER

DRINKING COKE

25 YEARS OLD

16 YEARS OLD

TO SEE IF YOU'VE FIGURED IT OUT, TURN TO PAGE 146 ...

Cheater-Detection

The correct answer for both versions of the task is that you have to turn over the first and last cards. Both tests have exactly the same logical form.

The fact that the same logical problem is easy in one context and hard in another suggests that the mind is not a single, general-purpose reasoning device, but rather a collection of special-purpose mechanisms.

Cosmides and Tooby did lots of control tests to eliminate other hypotheses. They found that people could only pass the test easily when it was framed in the context of a situation involving cheats.

So, if our ability to reason deductively evolved specifically to help us detect cheats and police social contracts, then we would expect that it would be easier to use deductive reasoning in the context of cheater-detection than in other contexts.

Two Features of Mental Modules

In order to follow the argument of Cosmides and Tooby, it is necessary to understand two important features of mental modules.

1.
Informational encapsulation.
Each module has its own rules for processing information, and its own knowledge base. A module does not have access to the rules or the knowledge base of another module.

2.
Domain specificity.
A module is only activated when relevant kinds of input are provided. Each module evolved to solve a particular adaptive problem, and is only activated when information relevant to that particular problem is supplied.

Modularity Again

Tooby and Cosmides claim that among the modules for regulating social exchange, there is a cheater-detection module. Some of the rules for deductive reasoning may be stored in this module. Like all modules, the cheater-detection module is informationally encapsulated, so other modules do not have access to the rule for deductive reasoning.

The first version of the Wason-selection task provided the information in an abstract form.

Reductionism

Another accusation often hurled at evolutionary psychology by its critics is that of "reductionism". The critics use this word as if it were a term of abuse, but in fact it refers to the basic procedure of all science. Science is all about explaining lots of apparently distinct phenomena in terms of a few underlying principles.

FOR EXAMPLE, NEWTON'S THEORY OF GRAVITY "REDUCES" THE MANY BIZARRE MOVEMENTS OF THE PLANETS AND STARS TO A SINGLE FORCE.

IT'S ALL DUE TO ONE THING – GRAVITY.

The Simplest Accurate Theory

There is nothing wrong with looking for simple theories, of course. What is wrong is pursuing simplicity at the expense of accuracy. Scientists seek *the simplest theory that is accurate* – not the simplest theory, full stop. If a scientist simplifies a theory so much that it can no longer explain all the data, that is not good science.

THE AMERICAN PHILOSOPHER **DANIEL DENNETT** REFERS TO THIS MISTAKE AS "GREEDY REDUCTIONISM", TO DISTINGUISH IT FROM REDUCTIONISM ITSELF, WHICH IS GOOD SCIENTIFIC PRACTICE.

REDUCTIONISM IS JUST GOOD SCIENCE. GREEDY REDUCTIONISM IS BAD SCIENCE.

Are evolutionary psychologists guilty of "greedy reductionism"? Evolutionary psychologists *are* reductionists, in the sense that they try to explain apparently distinct phenomena in terms of common principles. They deny being greedy reductionists, because they do not oversimplify the complex phenomena they are dealing with.

PSYCHOLOGY CAN BE REDUCED TO ONE BASIC PRINCIPLE: THE ASSOCIATION OF IDEAS.

THE MIND *CAN* BE UNDERSTOOD — BUT NOT JUST IN TERMS OF A *SINGLE* PRINCIPLE.

THE HUMAN MIND IS TOO COMPLEX TO BE FULLY UNDERSTOOD.

DAVID HUME (SCOTTISH PHILOSOPHER, 1711 – 1776)

PINKER

FODOR

Genetic Determinism

Some critics also accuse evolutionary psychologists of promoting "genetic determinism". What they mean by this phrase is that evolutionary psychologists place too much importance on genes and not enough on environment. The critics think that this leads evolutionary psychologists to believe that many human behaviours are inevitable and unchangeable.

There are three important problems with this line of reasoning. We shall look at each of them in turn. When we have examined them, we will see that the accusation of "genetic determinism" is entirely wrongheaded.

Is Too Much Importance Attached to Genes?

For hundreds of years, people have argued about whether human behaviour is the result of *nature* or *nurture*. On the side of nature, people like **Francis Galton** (1822-1911) argued that personality traits and cognitive differences are fixed at birth.

GENIUSES AND IDIOTS ARE BORN, NOT MADE.

HEREDITARY GENIUS
Francis Galton
1869

THESE ARGUMENTS WERE REJECTED BY OTHERS, WHO ARGUED THAT EVERYONE WAS BORN WITH THE SAME POTENTIAL.

GENES AREN'T EVERYTHING; THE ENVIRONMENT MATTERS TOO.

Nature vs. Nurture

With the advent of genetics in the 20th century, these competing theories were rephrased in scientific terms. "Nature" was equated with genetic causes and "nurture" was equated with environmental causes. But though the terminology changed, the arguments were the same. People continued to approach the debate as if it were an either/or issue.

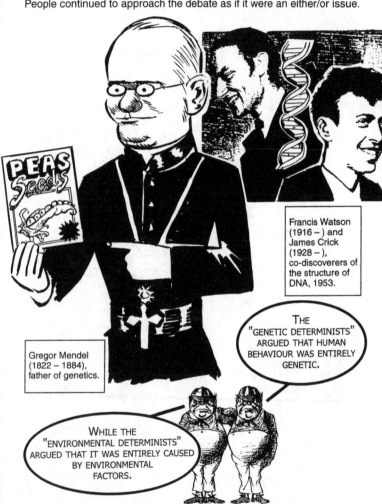

Francis Watson (1916 –) and James Crick (1928 –), co-discoverers of the structure of DNA, 1953.

Gregor Mendel (1822 – 1884), father of genetics.

THE "GENETIC DETERMINISTS" ARGUED THAT HUMAN BEHAVIOUR WAS ENTIRELY GENETIC.

WHILE THE "ENVIRONMENTAL DETERMINISTS" ARGUED THAT IT WAS ENTIRELY CAUSED BY ENVIRONMENTAL FACTORS.

Behavioural Genetics

In the 1960s, the science of behavioural genetics began to emerge as a way of testing these competing theories by using innovative methods such as twin-studies and adoption studies. Since then, behavioural geneticists have discovered that most psychological traits are influenced by a combination of both genetic *and* environmental factors, though the relative importance of each differs from trait to trait.

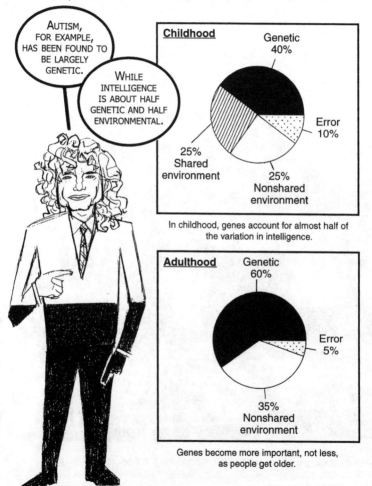

In childhood, genes account for almost half of the variation in intelligence.

Genes become more important, not less, as people get older.

Human Variation and Human Nature

When behavioural geneticists say that intelligence is "half genetic", they mean that about half of variation in intelligence scores of the people in a given range of environments can be attributed to genetic differences. But evolutionary psychologists are not really concerned with such individual differences. Unlike behavioural genetics, evolutionary psychology is concerned with the underlying **similarities** in human behaviour.

> PEOPLE HAVE DIFFERENTLY-SIZED HEARTS AND BRAINS, BUT THEY ALL HAVE HEARTS AND BRAINS.

> IN THE SAME WAY, PEOPLE HAVE DIFFERENTLY-"SIZED" MENTAL MODULES, BUT THEY ALL HAVE THE SAME BASIC MENTAL DESIGN.

Evolutionary psychologists are interested in the basic design features of the mind that all humans share – human nature.

Insofar as evolutionary psychologists say anything about the relative importance of genetic and environmental factors in causing individual differences, they accept the results of behavioural genetics. In other words, they accept that most traits are influenced by both genetic and environmental causes. Evolutionary psychologists stress the importance of understanding how genetic and environmental factors interact, and point out that genes often build different minds in response to different environments.

THIS IS A LONG WAY FROM GENETIC DETERMINISM!

Are Human Behaviours Inevitable and Unchangeable?

Evolutionary psychologists accept that it is possible to change most human behaviour. Every kind of behaviour results from the way in which our minds interact with our environment, and the mind results from the interaction of the environment with our genes. Different environments will lead the mind to develop differently and change the way in which the mind causes behaviour.

INDEED, THIS **FLEXIBILITY** IS AN IMPORTANT PART OF THE WAY WE ARE **DESIGNED**.

NATURAL SELECTION HAS PROGRAMMED HUMAN DEVELOPMENT TO BE CONTINGENT ON VARIOUS ENVIRONMENTAL TRIGGERS.

However, humans are not infinitely flexible. Changes in the environment still interact with a relatively stable genome and a relatively fixed mental architecture.

Does Evolutionary Psychology Justify the Status Quo?

Evolutionary psychology provides no moral justification for any political programme. Evolutionary psychology is a science, and science is about discovering facts, not about making value-judgements. A statement about the way in which humans *actually* behave may be true or false, but a claim about how humans *should* behave is neither true nor false – it is just a subjective opinion that stands alone.

JUST BECAUSE HUMANS DO IN FACT HAVE AN EVOLVED TENDENCY TO FAVOUR RELATIVES OVER NON-RELATIVES DOES NOT MEAN THAT NEPOTISM IS GOOD.

EVOLUTIONARY PSYCHOLOGY DESCRIBES WHAT HUMAN NATURE IS LIKE – IT DOES NOT PRESCRIBE WHAT HUMANS SHOULD DO.

The Naturalistic Fallacy

Arguing that something is good because it is natural is called the "naturalistic fallacy". It is based on the mistaken idea that you can deduce moral lessons from observing nature.

The sciences, including evolutionary psychology, restrict themselves to making factual claims, and leave the business of value-judgements to ethics. Ethical questions cannot be settled by science. Perhaps this is the key to human freedom.

Mistaken Criticisms and Misunderstandings

The accusations of "genetic determinism" that some critics level at evolutionary psychology are completely unfounded. Evolutionary psychology does not place too much importance on genes.

The Legacy of History

The answer lies with history. Darwin's ideas about evolution have been distorted by many people in an attempt to justify various political projects, some of which have been truly evil. For example, in Victorian times, **Herbert Spencer** (1820-1903) and other "social Darwinists" (as they were known) thought they could find support in Darwin's ideas for their ruthless *laissez-faire* economic policies.

In Germany in the 1930s and 40s, the Nazis looked to Darwin to justify their racist eugenic policies, which culminated in the extermination of millions of Jews during the Second World War.

The social Darwinists and the Nazi eugenicists claimed that their policies were rooted in Darwinian theory, but this is a gross error. Darwin never claimed that his theories justified social inequality or eugenic policies. However, the mud stuck. After the Second World War, any mention of evolutionary theory in connection with human psychology automatically tended to make people recall the atrocities of Nazi Germany. Today, many people react the same way to evolutionary psychology, even though evolutionary psychologists have gone to great lengths to distance themselves from the evils of social Darwinism and Nazi eugenics. The critics of evolutionary psychology may be wrong in accusing it of genetic determinism, but their fears become more understandable in the light of history.

The Future of Evolutionary Psychology

Evolutionary psychologists have responded to these fears in two ways. On the one hand, they remind the critics that they are only attempting to describe what human nature is like, not to prescribe what humans should do. On the other hand, they argue that the discoveries of evolutionary psychology could be used to inform left-wing policies just as much as, if not more than, right-wing policies. For example, policy-makers who wish to promote a more equal distribution of wealth might take heart from the finding that humans are adapted to live in groups in which inequality is relatively low.

PETER SINGER, CONTEMPORARY MORAL PHILOSOPHER.

Evolutionary psychology is still in its infancy. Even though Darwin's theory of evolution has been around for over a century, it was not until the 1970s that psychologists began to see the relevance of evolutionary theory for understanding the human mind. As with any new science, some of the first studies had serious flaws. But evolutionary psychologists have learned from these mistakes, and more recent studies have been much more sophisticated.

The Darwinian Revolution

In the last ten years especially, evolutionary psychology has made great progress. Each year, more and more studies have appeared that confirm evolutionary hypotheses about the human mind. Many commentators have remarked that a new paradigm is being born.

The Darwinian Model makes more accurate predictions and integrates our knowledge of humans with the rest of our scientific knowledge.

The Future of Psychology

In the future, the study of human psychology will be completely transformed by the Darwinian approach. Just as we have learned much about the human body by studying the selective processes that "designed" it, so we are learning much about the human mind by studying its evolutionary history. In the words of George Williams …

Further Reading

Two very good introductions to evolutionary psychology are recommended.

How the Mind Works, by Steven Pinker (UK: Penguin, 1998; US: Norton, 1997). Over 600 pages, but an easy-to-read introduction by one of the pioneers of evolutionary psychology.

The Moral Animal: Evolutionary Psychology and Everyday Life, by Robert Wright (UK: Abacus, 1995; US: Pantheon, 1994). Slightly shorter than Pinker's book and more informal. Illustrates lots of evolutionary psychology with examples from Darwin's life, so you get a potted biography of Darwin too!

For primary sources, try some of the following pioneering studies in evolutionary psychology.

Homicide, by Martin Daly and Margo Wilson (Aldine de Gruyter, 1988). Reveals the cross-cultural patterns in homicide data and provides a Darwinian explanation.

The Evolution of Desire: Strategies of Human Mating, by David Buss (UK: HarperCollins, 1994; US: Basic Books, 1994). Examines the different sexual strategies of men and women from an evolutionary perspective. Based on the massive survey that Buss conducted, involving 10,000 people from 33 countries.

The Adapted Mind: Evolutionary Psychology and the Generation of Culture, edited by Jerome Barkow, Leda Cosmides and John Tooby (Oxford University Press, 1992). Classic collection of original studies, including the famous study by Cosmides and Tooby about cheater-detection. Style and format are rather academic, but the arguments are compelling.

Handbook of Evolutionary Psychology, edited by Charles Crawford and David Krebs (Lawrence Erlbaum Associates, 1997). A more recent collection of original papers. Quite technical. Not for the beginner.

For some of the basic biological theory underlying evolutionary psychology, you couldn't do better than read the following.

The Selfish Gene, by Richard Dawkins (Oxford University Press, 1989). First published in 1976, this book popularized the discoveries of

George Williams, William Hamilton, Robert Trivers and other evolutionary biologists. It remains one of the most important contributions to contemporary Darwinian thinking.

The Blind Watchmaker, also by Richard Dawkins (UK: Penguin, 1988; US: Norton, 1988). Gives a very clear account of how natural selection works and corrects many common misunderstandings.

The Ant and the Peacock, by Helena Cronin (Cambridge University Press, 1992). Describes how evolutionary biologists solved some important puzzles by developing the fascinating theories of kin selection, reciprocal altruism and the theory of sexual selection.

For information about our human and hominid ancestors, try the following.

The Day Before Yesterday: Five Million Years of Human History, by Colin Tudge (UK: Jonathan Cape, 1995; US: (*The Time Before History*) Scribner, 1996). A good survey of human evolution by one of the finest contemporary science-writers.

Humans Before Humanity: An Evolutionary Perspective, by Robert Foley (Blackwell, 1997). A more academic look at the palaeontological record.

And here are two excellent books on the evolution of language.

The Language Instinct: The New Science of Language and Mind, by Steven Pinker (UK: Penguin, 1994; US: William Morrow, 1994). Summarizes the latest developments in linguistics and sets these discoveries in the context of evolutionary theory.

Grooming, Gossip and the Evolution of Language, by Robin Dunbar (UK: Faber, 1996; US: Harvard University Press, 1997). Dunbar explains his theory that language first evolved as a means of swapping social information.

Finally, the *Darwinism Today* series (edited by Helena Cronin and Oliver Curry, and published by Weidenfeld and Nicholson in the UK and Yale University Press in the US) explores new developments in evolutionary psychology in short, highly readable essays.

Evolutionary Psychology Journals

Books are always a few years behind the latest research. For the most up-to-date work in any science, you need to consult scholarly journals. Evolutionary psychology is well served in this respect with two journals dedicated exclusively to work in this field: *Evolution and Human Behavior* (formerly *Ethology and Sociobiology*) is published bi-monthly by Elsevier Science, and *Human Nature* is published quarterly by Aldine de Gruyter. Many important papers on evolutionary psychology can also be found in *Behavioral and Brain Sciences*, which is published quarterly by Cambridge University Press.

Evolutionary Psychology on the Internet

the evolutionist is a site containing interviews with leading evolutionary thinkers. You can find it on the web at:
http://www.lse.ac.uk/cpnss/evolutionist

You can also visit the website of the Human Behavior and Evolution Society at:
http://psych.lmu.edu/hbes.htm

The Authors

Dylan Evans is a research student in the Department of Philosophy, Logic and Scientific Method at the London School of Economics. He is writing his PhD about cognitive science and the emotions.

Oscar Zarate has illustrated six other Icon *Introducing* titles: *Freud, Stephen Hawking, Quantum Theory, Machiavelli, Melanie Klein* and *Mind & Brain*, as well as *Lenin for Beginners* and *Mafia for Beginners*. He has also produced many acclaimed graphic novels, including *A Small Killing*, which won the Will Eisner Prize for the best graphic novel of 1994, and has edited *It's Dark in London*, a collection of graphic stories, published in 1996.

Acknowledgements

The author would like to thank Helena Cronin and Oliver Curry for reading various drafts of the manuscript and providing invaluable constructive criticism. Thanks are also due to Richard Appignanesi and Oscar Zarate for their suggestions and for helping to make the book such fun to write. Last but not least, thanks to all those who supplied photos of themselves and other people for Oscar to work with.

The artist would like to thank Judy Groves and Joe Rainer for their technical help and extends his gratitude to Miguel Zarate for his valuable support.

Oscar dedicates his part of this work to the memory of his mother Antonia.

Index